POSITIVE
MINDSET HABITS
FOR TEACHERS

Also by the Author:

Positive Mindset Journal for Teachers (3 editions)

The Happy Habit: 10 Simple Habits - Step By Step Guide To Finding More Happiness & Joy in Your Life

Mindfulness Meditation for Beginners: From Zero to Zen in Ten - A No-Nonsense Starter Guide for Seekers and Skeptics

Stop Procrastinating: 9 Simple Habits Step By Step - How to Regain Control of Your Time and Your Life in One Fun Filled Week

POSITIVE

MINDSET HABITS

FOR TEACHERS

10 STEPS TO REDUCE STRESS,
INCREASE STUDENT ENGAGEMENT and
REIGNITE YOUR PASSION FOR TEACHING

Grace Stevens

Positive Mindset Habits for Teachers – 10 Steps to Reduce Stress, Increase Student Engagement and Reignite Your Passion for Teaching

Copyright © 2018 by Grace Stevens

Red Lotus Books

Mountain House CA

Red Lotus Books

Note: Some names and situations have been altered to protect those known to the author.

Cover design by Rocio Martin Osuna

ISBN : 978-0-9987019-4-3

Printed in the USA

http://www.happy-classrooms.com.com

First Edition: May 2018

Contents

S p e c i a l   G i f t

Grab the Workbook and Six Week Journal

To get the most out of this book, please print out and use the free workbook. It includes exercises and worksheets pertaining to the book. It is available for download at www.happy-classrooms.com/workbook. You can also download a six-week version of the Positive Mindset Journal for Teachers free of charge. The journal is the perfect tool to help you practice your happy mindset habits.

If you are reading the digital version of this book, simply click this link. If you are reading a print version, please visit:

www.happy-classrooms.com/workbook

The Elephant in the Classroom

"Tell me, what is it you plan to do
With your one wild and precious life?"

"The Summer Day" by Mary Oliver

This is likely not the first book to begin with this beautiful question from Mary Oliver. But it may well be the first where the readers already know the answer. What we have chosen to do with our one wild and precious life is this - teach.

So a deeper question surfaces - how can we be happier with our choice? Those beautiful Pinterest images of coordinated classrooms, creative, fun lesson plans, and motivational quotes disguise a sad reality of the teaching profession today. In actuality, many teachers are constantly stressed, overwhelmed and exhausted. Increasing numbers are leaving the profession, and many who stay are resentful and disillusioned. Hardly the stuff of happy classrooms and joyful, meaningful learning experiences.

The following pages are aimed at providing a roadmap to answer that question. If you were drawn to this book, you presumably plan on staying in teaching. The challenges that face education are real and are many. There are no quick fixes. I don't need to list the reasons for teachers' disillusionment here; we are already too painfully aware of them. Some challenges in education may be here to stay for a while, but so are we. Therefore, the predicament then becomes how to take responsibility for our happiness so that we can continue with this noble career. I believe teaching can be a rewarding and meaningful career. It's a profession that has not only the potential to shape the future, but also to make us happy while doing so. Let me show you how.

This may be one of the few books you read that is just for teachers. That might sound like an exaggeration when in all likelihood you have at least ten of them on the shelf behind your desk at school. But if you blow the dust off them you will notice that they are about teaching - teaching strategies, classroom management, student engagement, learning styles, language acquisition, learning difficulties, mindset theory. In addition to the books, I'm guessing you also have binders from professional development days. Are any of these written just for you, aimed purely at making your experience in the classroom a more positive one? Probably not. This book is for teachers, not students and not test scores (although all of these things will improve as a result of your happiness). This book is for you.

We are at a critical point. Not only are talented educators burning out and fleeing from this profession at an alarming rate, but there is also a shortage of recruits in the wings ready to take on the challenges and responsibility of teaching other people's children. Combine this with the fact that students learn best in a happy classroom, focusing on putting a little more "happy" in your teaching day is suddenly not only a worthwhile goal but a professional responsibility.

We know that a happy classroom is an essential key to not only a positive school culture and less teacher burnout but also to increased student engagement and student success. Positively focused brains have been proven to be 31% more productive than a negatively, neutrally or stressed brain. "Happy" brains show increases in energy, creativity, and intelligence. According to the research of Sean Achor, professor of Positive Psychology at Harvard and the author of *The Happiness Advantage,*

"Positive emotions flood our brains with dopamine and serotonin, chemicals that not only make us feel good but dial up the learning centers of our brains to higher levels. They help us organize new information, keep that information in the brain longer, and retrieve it faster later on. And they enable us to make and sustain more neural connections, which allows us to think more quickly and creatively, become more skilled at complex analysis and problem solving, and see and invent new ways of doing things."

Achor's research was based on adults, but it also holds true for children.

Now I'll admit, I'm a neuro nerd. I understand that brain research might not excite everyone as it does me. But as it turns out, you don't need me or any amount of research to convince you that happy teachers are more effective than stressed and overwhelmed ones. Your own experience not only as a teacher but also as a child who attended school will tell you that this is true.

In the Workbook, you will find an exercise where you reflect on your favorite learning experiences. If this isn't something you have considered in a while, it can be valuable to take some time to complete it. Contemplating these questions will lead you to the same conclusion.

Take a moment to think back to your favorite grade school teacher. Close your eyes and think about this. What was it that made them your favorite teacher? Picture them in front of you. What were they doing, saying? What was the overall atmosphere of the class? Chances are your teacher had an energy about them that was in control, yet relaxed. They made learning fun and engaging. It's likely you'll remember the activities you participated in more than the actual curriculum taught. Words that usually come up when I ask people to describe their favorite teacher are "passionate," "fun," "interested in us." People tend to remember more how they felt in class, less what they learned. And how they felt in class was safe, valued, engaged … happy.

Now think about high school or even higher education. What were your favorite classes, who were the professors who made an impact? What was it about these experiences that made them stand out? While we may think we want the class that guarantees "an easy A," the classes and professors we remember and value most are the ones that challenged yet excited us. Professors who were passionate about what they were teaching and who brought high yet positive expectations to our learning experience.

Now think of your own experiences teaching. Please be very honest with yourself (this isn't an assignment you are going to turn in for grading or judgment). Think about the days when you are a teaching rockstar. The days when teaching seems fun. Likely in this scenario, the students are engaged and compliant. You feel connected and passionate about the creative ways you are presenting the material. You are patient and look at tangents and misunderstanding as learning opportunities. You feel so privileged that spending time with inquiring minds is how you get to spend your day. You know, the type of days you assumed would be the norm when you showed up with that shiny new teaching credential.

Now compare this positive teaching image to the days when you are feeling overwhelmed in your classroom. You are stressed, frustrated at the monotony of the curriculum, maybe a little underprepared. Students are acting out and teaching just seems like drudgery. It's OK to admit you have those days. None of us are perfect; we've all been there. Unfortunately, you may well know teachers who permanently live in that space. The point of this exercise is not to make you feel bad about yourself or your teaching. It's not to point fingers; it's to get you to pose this question - in which scenario do you suppose the students are engaged and learning? With rockstar teacher, or burnt-out teacher?

No need to quote research, you already know the answer. As a teacher, your energy speaks louder than your words. Students respond directly to the energy bring to the classroom.

Are you happy to be in your profession, passionate about teaching and looking for ways to make it fun? Or are you focused on all of the issues that make teaching increasingly more challenging. Are you visibly frustrated and overwhelmed and counting the days until summer vacation? Students pick up on your energy, regardless of what you are saying. The extent to which students learn and have a successful day has less to do with the adopted curriculum, access to technology or class size, and more to do with whether they like us, want to please us, are happy to be in the classroom and believe that we are too. That's a reality. And that's why, as teachers, we need to find ways to have more moments of connection and joy in the classroom. We need to be happier not just for our sakes, but as a professional responsibility to our students. But how?

Here's the good news. Happiness can be synthesized. Becoming "happier" is a skill you can learn, and a set of habits you can practice. And teaching is the ideal profession in which to practice these happy habits.

When I became a public school teacher in the early 2000's, I was making a conscious decision to live a happier life. I was fifteen years into a corporate career where I had achieved most of the professional and financial goals I had set for myself. I was a VP; I traveled to fun places, I made great money. By all traditional standards, I was living the American Dream. And yet I was stressed, disconnected from my family and saw little value in what I was doing.

When I started teaching, I felt like I had won the lottery. Well, not financially, of course, but in many other ways. To anyone who asked I cited three reasons - being a public school teacher is important, teaching comes easily to me, and it makes me happy. Or more specifically, my classroom was a place I found it easy to experience happy moments.

Unwittingly I had stumbled on a career that had many of the key components to synthesizing happiness. Martin Seligman, the founding father of the science of positive psychology, proposes that "happiness" can be broken into five measurable building blocks - pleasure, engagement, meaning, relationships and accomplishment. Teaching has the potential to provide all of these in abundance.

Let's look at these in the context of teaching. First, the potential to be in "flow" state, or deeply engaged in what you are doing. Anyone who has ever spent even a few hours in a classroom setting is aware of how all-consuming the process of teaching is, allowing little opportunity for thoughts to wonder. Next, teaching is an "honorable" profession, providing an essential service. So our day has meaning.

15

Additionally, it provides many opportunities for connection and community (relationships). Finally, in an ideal world, teachers have the freedom in their classroom to be creative and have fun with students (pleasure and accomplishment).

So from a theoretical standpoint, at least, teachers have indeed won the "happiness" lottery. Yet step into any school staff room, and an atmosphere of joy, fulfillment, collaboration and flow state does not usually greet you at the door. More likely, you will be met by a group of well-meaning and exhausted individuals who wear the culture of being overworked, underpaid, and underappreciated like a badge of honor. We're teachers. It's what we do.

Now I'll be honest, I was naively optimistic when I got into teaching. As a "second career" teacher, I know what several well-paying but soul draining careers look like up close and personal. I still remember the excitement I felt getting the keys to my very own classroom, the care I took setting up the room, purchasing supplies, organizing every detail down to picking out my first-day outfit. Even though I wasn't a bright and shiny twenty-something with a new credential and no real world experience, I still had naively unrealistic expectations. In my mind teaching would be a walk in the park. I was an adult, a parent, someone who has lived through some tough circumstances, who had solid life experience under their belt. How hard could it be to decorate a room all cute, read some classic literature, and spend my day with young, inquiring minds? Oh, and have summers off to hang with my kids. Pretty darn hard, as it turned out.

After fifteen years, that excitement of that first set of keys has been replaced by a quiet satisfaction and confidence that my classroom is a place where good things happen, and learning occurs. I value my classroom as a place of fun, creativity and positivity, a space where everyone feels safe, respected, and challenged. A place where we have many happy moments. And essentially that's what a happy life is - one in which you string together a sequence of happy moments and savor them. Despite the many challenges, I still feel that when I chose to become a teacher I won the jackpot. I would like to hand you a winning lottery ticket, too.

In 2013 I wrote a book called *The Happy Habit - 10 Simple Steps to Find More Happiness in Your Life*. Based on the science of positive psychology and my twenty-year journey in learning how to synthesize happiness, the book shared practical tips on how to be more joyful. I wanted to title the book *Happy Comes First*. People told me that it sounded a little "woo-woo" (we can take that to mean "New age and not in a good way.") Now we have the science to back up what I have long proposed - success comes when we are happier and more positive, not the other way around. We need to be happy first. So I return to my earlier statement. There is good news here, being happy is a set of habits that you can learn and practice. And teaching is the ideal arena in which to do so.

From a purely pragmatic standpoint, as individual teachers, we do not have a lot of control over many of the major challenges in education today. But reconnecting with the joy and passion that we imagined for ourselves when we entered this noble profession, this is TOTALLY in our control.

This we can fix. And if we remain open to the idea that we need to change ourselves before we can change our world (be happy first), then the ideas in this book can provide an excellent and relatively pain-free roadmap.

Is there an easy formula for happiness? In his best-selling book *The Happiness Advantage* Jonathan Haidt proposes the following:

$$H = S + C + V$$

In his formula Happiness equals Setpoint (our natural predisposition to be positively or negatively focused) plus Conditioning (work, engagement, flow state, and connections with others) and Voluntary Activities. The Happy Habits in this book are precisely these voluntary activities. They are activities and mindsets we consciously engage in that boost our happiness level. They can be learned, they can be practiced, and they can dramatically increase our happiness quotient. Flexing our "happy muscles" can change our brain, our outlook, and our experiences.

Give the ideas in this book 30 days. Six school weeks. Unless you got this book at the very end of the school year, you are going to be in school for the next six weeks, anyway. What can it hurt? You don't need to make a big deal about it. You don't need to join a Facebook support group or report out to a cohort. This is your personal business and challenge. Download the six-week version of the Positive Mindset Journal and commit to writing in it daily. It takes less than 5 minutes. Here's the link again, or go to www.happy-classrooms.com/workbook and click on the "Six-Week Journal" icon.

There are ten mindset habits in all. In each chapter, I will go over the science and rationale for the mindset, and then provide a specific list of actions you can take in your classroom to practice it.

None of the strategies require any money. They do involve a modest amount of time and, of course, a shift in mindset. * I invite you to take on the challenge of being happier for yourself, as you deserve to enjoy your day. And if you are one of those teachers who gives blood, sweat, tears, and devotion to your class to the point of exhaustion, if you won't do it for yourself, do it for your students. Students need positive role models and positive environments in which to learn. We know this.

As there are lots of strategies in this book, trying them all at once may be over-ambitious. I suggest trying a few until they become a habit and you are comfortable incorporating them into your day. Then add a few more to your repertoire. If a couple of them don't appeal to you, skip them, there are plenty of others you can try. Six weeks should be long enough to feel a subtle change in your energy and your mood. How much happier will you be? It's hard to quantify. The effect is cumulative. A little less stress, a little more joy, a few more moments of inspiration, connection, creativity, and quiet satisfaction. Don't worry about the details right now. Just accept and expect that you can be happier.

Come with me and let me show you how.

* A side note with regards to mindset

I would be remiss not to thank Dr. Carol Dweck for doing a lot of the heavy lifting for me in this area. Due to the current popularity of her research on Growth Mindset, I find that educators, in particular, are a lot more receptive to the basic idea that our brains are like muscles that can be improved with exercise, and that connectivity between neurons can be changed by experience and habits of thought. Just as our intelligence isn't fixed, neither is our happiness set point. I am eternally indebted to Dr. Dweck for bringing this critical idea to education. It has been a thrill to hear conversations in classrooms change and see report card grades amended from an "N" ("not achieved") to "NY" ("not achieved yet"). On a personal note, it also makes my ideas seem a lot more mainstream. No woo-woo here, friends.

Choose It, Don't Chase It

"Happiness is not a pursuit; it's a perspective."

Kristine Carlson, Co-Author of the *Don't Sweat the Small Stuff* Book Series

Time magazine runs entire issues about it. Harvard University has classes on it. The US army trains its Westpoint cadets in it. The science of being happy is big news and big business. And yet there is so little emphasis on it in mainstream public education. Think about it, have you ever participated in a professional development day devoted to how to be happy as a teacher?

Here's the sum of my experience in this area. One five minute discussion on "avoiding burnout in your first year of teaching" when I was finishing up my credential program. It was true that the first year of teaching was insanely busy.

There was so much to learn, so much to plan and also a lot of adjustments to be made in realigning some of my naive expectations. I am embarrassed but also rather amused to recall how utterly shocked I was to discover that not every student coming into my grade had the prerequisite skills. "What do you mean they can't read at grade level? Why weren't they held back?" It does seem laughable now. But I expected the first year to be hard, and I still had that amazing excitement level and gratitude to be involved in teaching to counterbalance the crazy workload and expectations adjustment.

Talking to teachers now, especially veteran ones, it does seem that education is getting more stressful every year. I don't think it's because we are getting old and less patient. If anything, I seemed to have developed a better sense of perspective and more patience over the years. So logically it would seem that it should be getting easier. And many aspects of teaching have gotten easier. I have learned that helping students who struggle, even though it takes a lot of energy, is ultimately one of the most satisfying parts of the job. I am at peace with the fact that not all students learn the same way and on the same day. I accept that just because I taught something (even if I spent hours on the lesson plan, made it engaging and delivered it flawlessly, thank you very much), it does not mean that students learned it. I have a good repertoire of classroom management skills so that behavior issues don't phase me as much as they used to. I have established a solid reputation and working relationship with colleagues and many parents in the school community. I have developed a rhythm, voice, and confidence in my teaching style. And yet the stress is cumulative. It seems to get greater every year, not less.

So it turns out that the first year of teaching wasn't the problem. I'd compare it to that first year or marriage that everyone said would be the hardest. While the first year of marriage can surely be a big adjustment, we were still in our honeymoon phase, excited to be playing house and willing to overlook so many little annoyances. It's two decades into the thing, when those issues continue to pile on and on to almost breaking point, that we start asking ourselves, "Is this really what I had in mind when I signed up for this?" and, "Is this really how I want to spend the rest of my life?"

I love teaching and find joy and peace being in my classroom and with my students. But if I don't proactively focus on remaining positive and looking for joyful moments of my day, I could easily succumb to the "dark side". You know, turn into the teacher who corrects papers and tests in staff meetings and spends their down time reposting snarky memes on social media about how awful teaching, students, administrators and parents are. The teacher who starts the "days until summer" countdown the minute winter break is over.

I don't need to tell you all the ways our jobs are overwhelming and stressful. Or ponder why staff meetings and professional development days seem specifically designed to suck the joy out of us. You are already painfully too aware of the reasons or you would not have found your way to this book. But my point is this. We need to take responsibility for own happiness and job satisfaction. Despite what we know about the direct correlation between happy teachers, school culture, and student success, administrators and districts are also under incredible stress. They do not have our happiness on their radar or in their professional development budget. You are going to have to take ownership of your happiness initiative. I've told you why it's so important for your students. Here's why it's crucial for you.

Just a few of the proven benefits of being happier are:

- decreased blood pressure
- decreased incidence of heart disease
- improved immunity response
- increased longevity
- increased energy, productivity, and creativity

That's not a list of benefits to take lightly. It's not just our job fulfillment at stake; it's our health.

So here's the first strategy. Decide that being happy in your teaching day is your top priority. Understand that finding ways to cultivate joy in your day and savor those moments should be the top goal on your list of things you need to accomplish. Because if we dig deep enough into any of the items on that list and ask yourself why we want to accomplish any of them, we will likely get to the end result of, "Because it will make me happy." It doesn't matter if the goal is to work less, have greater financial freedom, have more rewarding relationships, live in a nicer house or work for a better school district. Everything we want we essentially want because we think we will feel better in the having of it. Being happier is the goal.

So far, so good. We can all agree that we want to be happy. But here's the big mindset shift that needs to take place. Most people view happiness as some future event. They have the idea that they'll be happy when something changes. We need to get on board with the idea that we can be happy now, in our current circumstances. That's right, not when we get "better students," the grade assignment we want, more responsible parents, more supportive administrators, more professional and harder working colleagues, more prep time, not when we have tenure, or even when we retire. We cannot keep putting off being happier as a future event contingent on having that mythical "perfect class." We need to decide that we will be happier now, in the situation we have.

Well here's some good news regarding this - science is on our side. The research demonstrates that only 10% of our "happiness quotient" is dictated by our life circumstances. At first, that number seems impossibly low, right? But this has been repeatedly proven.

Let's examine some theories about this that you may have heard about before. Dan Gilbert explores them in depth in his book *Stumbling on Happiness*. But I can summarize. The first idea is the theory of "hedonic adaptation."

In a famous 1978 study, the "happiness" level of two groups of participants was measured. The first group had won the lottery. The actual big money lottery, not my "isn't teaching amazing" lottery. The second group had suffered traumatic injuries that had resulted in paralysis.

Clearly, we would expect the first group of participants, the lottery winners, to have a lot more to be happy about than the folks who had become paralyzed. And in the first few months, this was certainly the case. But in both cases, the euphoria of winning the lottery and the devastation of being paralyzed was relatively short-lived. Within about six months participants in both groups had returned to their "default" or natural happiness level, the same level they experienced before the life-changing events. This default level depended more on their natural disposition and perspective than their actual circumstances. These findings suggest that we are genetically hard-wired to adapt to a variety of life situations, good and bad, and we tend to overestimate the effect that external circumstances will have on our dispositions.

At first, I was a little skeptical about these findings. But other studies over the years have yielded the same results. The only two circumstances that take years for people to "bounce back" from are the death of loved ones, or the loss of a career followed by a long period of unemployment. Other than these two situations, most of us "reset" to our natural happiness level relatively quickly, even after a change in circumstances that we thought would have been hugely impactful.

A recent documentary on happiness featured a young man who became paralyzed after a diving accident. He explains that even though he was depressed in the months immediately following the accident, he returned to his "normal self" within a few months after he had a chance to adapt to his new life in a wheelchair. He points out this ability to use his limbs, while important, wasn't his whole life. He still had a loving family, he still had the same friends, laughed at the same jokes, enjoyed the same food. He still connected with people in meaningful ways and engaged in work that he believed was important.

A counterpart to the "hedonic adaptation" model is the "hedonic treadmill" model. Research indicates that we tend to overestimate the extent to which money and material possessions will make us happy. Don't get me wrong, being broke is very stressful, I don't think anyone will argue with that. But studies show that once your basic needs such as having adequate food, shelter and a means to provide for those you love are met, the difference that having an extra $500 in the bank makes to your happiness level versus having an extra $500,000 is negotiable. A Gallup poll of more than 600,000 Americans found there is significant fluctuation in the life satisfaction and happiness level of households with an annual income of less than $60,000. But for those with an annual income of over $60,000 (the amount presumably required to adequately meet those basic needs stress-free) the life satisfaction and happiness level is completely flat. That's the crux of the theory of hedonic adaptation. It appears that as our income increases, so do our expectations. We think that the great new pair of shoes, or the fancy new technology in our classroom, will make us happy. They will, for a while. But as we quickly adapt to our new acquisitions, we need new stimuli to give us the same flood of good feelings. We're on the hedonic treadmill.

There is one exception where money can make us happy, and that is when we spend it on experiences that connect us with others (travel, adventures, learning new things together). I will cover that in a later chapter. But for now just recognize that even though teaching is not a top paying industry, as long as our basic household needs are being met the salary should not be a major reason for unhappiness.

I am not suggesting that we shouldn't work on improving our life circumstances. I still participate in the teacher PowerBall pool every time it's a huge number and spend happy hours with my colleagues contemplating if we would all call in rich together, or take the high road and finish out the school year. It's good to want to improve our lives. But what if we could choose to have more happiness, joy, and peace in our current circumstances? Wouldn't we prefer that over still being stressed, overwhelmed and unhappy in new circumstances? Probably so. So the solution is to change our perspective (mindset) and our habits, not our circumstances.

The irony is that once we are happier, it will be easier for us to change those circumstances. With better balance and a more positive outlook, we are better able to reframe perceptions that might have been limiting us; we feel more empowered to take control of our success. Life somehow becomes smoother and easier. Again, happy needs to come first.

So if our external circumstances such as finances, health, status, and possessions only account for 10% of our happiness quotient, what makes up the other 90%?

Well, 50% depends on genetics. Remember the natural happiness set point that I talked about? There is a strong biological component to our predisposition to being optimistic and resilient and joyful. We all know people who seem to "bounce back" easily no matter what life throws at them. Conversely, we also know people who are never happy, no matter how well things appear to be unfolding for them. For reasons that scientists don't understand yet, some people are genetically predisposed to be happier than others. But just because you didn't win what Jonathan Haidt refers to as "the cortisol lottery," it doesn't mean that we can't learn to be happier. Just like having a predisposition for diabetes or heart disease doesn't necessarily mean you are doomed to get the disease, there are lifestyle choices we can make to increase our chances of having a happier life.

If you've kept up with the math, we have accounted for 60% of your happiness quotient. The last 40%? That's where we can game the system. The final 40% is what researchers refer to as "intentional activities." That's right, my happy mindset habits! There are certain activities and ways of thinking that people can engage in that will boost their happiness quotient. Some people naturally do these things, others have learned them. Likewise, there are patterns of thinking and habits that people engage in that prolong their misery. The trick is being aware of the positive habits, and start practicing them consistently.

I think now might be the time to take a quick timeout to define for yourself what happiness is. I can tell you what the dictionary and the experts say happiness is, but it will be more meaningful if you define it for yourself. There is an exercise in the workbook to help you with this. If you can, take a moment to complete it now. Here's the link to download the workbook if you haven't done so already. Or go to www.happy-classrooms.com/workbook

You may find it hard to describe what happiness is. Sometimes it's easier to recognize it by what it's not. For most people, happiness is the opposite of being stressed, overwhelmed, easily bothered, defensive, resentful, low energy, lacking interest, feeling disconnected or dissatisfied and feeling powerless to change things. That "Is it Friday yet?" feeling, when in reality we also suspect that our weekend doesn't have too much to look forward to other than getting caught up on sleep and work and maybe a couple of loads of laundry.

Defining happiness can be tricky - it's hard to describe, but we know it when we feel it.

There are a lot of things we look forward to doing that we think will bring us happiness. These can include finally getting home from work and watching our favorite TV shows or sporting events or kicking back with a glass of wine or a beer. Shopping, social media browsing. While none of these activities are bad, they are more of a distraction than actual "happiness." Excitement is also great (think of the rush of euphoria you feel when your favorite team scores a goal) but it is short lived. I love roller coaster rides, but I wouldn't want to stay on one for an hour. It's that sudden rush that makes it fun. Getting emotionally involved in a TV drama can serve a helpful function to enable us to decompress and forget about our troubles for a while, but I don't think that anyone would argue that binge-watching the latest season of Stranger Things is going to bring a deep sense of contentment to our lives.

You know that moment when you are outside doing something, and the sun or a cool breeze strokes your face, and you just have an overwhelming feeling of well-being for no real reason? That's happiness for me. A feeling of contentment and presence and not wanting anything in the current moment to be any different than it is. A calm inner peace and contentment and a sense of connection with others and something greater than myself. It can be that moment when my class suddenly "gets" a concept we've been working on, and they are happily engaged, working together. For that tiny, perfect, moment I step back and breathe it all in and I make a conscious effort to savor it. You know, like the song says, "If you're happy and you know it., clap your hands!" For me, that's the trick. The pursuit of a "happy life" can be pretty fruitless and frustrating. But looking for and savoring the mini miracles in my day, precious moments that fill me with well-being and happiness and savoring them? That seems very doable. And ultimately a "happy life" is a life where enough of these joy-filled moments stack up to make that difference in my perspective, my energy, and my disposition. I'm happy, and I know it. And life just seems to go easier all the way around.

So this is the foundation and the first happy mindset habit. Recognize that, even if we don't have a "glass half full" natural disposition, there are many intentional things we can do to boost our happiness quotient. Science has proven it again and again. Our job is now to be what I like to call a "Joy Detective." We are going to learn how to proactively seek and savor awesome moments in your day. The very first step is to make the intention to do so.

Recap of This Happiness Mindset Habit:

Happiness is a state of consciousness, not a circumstance. While each of us has a predetermined genetic "set point" for happiness, only 10% of our happiness quotient is based on our life circumstances. Almost half of our happiness quotient is made up of intentional behaviors and habits that we can learn - things that we have in our control. Once we accept that happiness is a muscle that can be exercised, we can make being happier an actionable goal and can commit to working on it every day.

Ways to Practice This Mindset Habit Starting Today:

1. Do you feel compelled to start with a benchmark? As teachers, we love our assessments and tracking progress, right? I'm only half joking. As this first habit deals almost exclusively with mindset, some of you "action-oriented" types might need something more tangible to work on.

You can indeed take a happiness survey to set a benchmark for yourself.

2. Here is the link to the University of Pennsylvania Authentic Happiness website. On their website you can take a whole battery of Positive Psychology tests such as "An Authentic Happiness Inventory", an "Optimism Test", relationship and life satisfaction questionnaires. To find the website just search "University of Pennsylvania Authentic Happiness"

3. Are you a To Do List maker? Commit to making the first action item on your To Do List "To look for things that make me happy today and savor them." Or, if you are concerned that others might look at your list and judge, just go with "JD." Your new day job is now to be a Joy Detective.

4. Take an honest look at your daily routines and schedules. Working in your "happiness habits" is going to take a small time investment. No more than 30 minutes a day once you make them part of your routine. If you are already feeling stressed and overwhelmed trying to get everything done, you will need to get creative to carve out ten minutes, three times a day. Decide how you can accomplish this. Like the old maxim says, "What gets scheduled, gets done." If you get up 10 minutes earlier, escape to your car or your classroom for the last 10 minutes of lunch, volunteer to get out of the house for 10 minutes a day walking the dog or simply walking around the neighborhood, you will be in good shape. Many of us just

do not have any more minutes to squeeze out of our day. Here's another saying, "You can't save time, you can only spend it." The question is, are you spending it wisely? Carpool, cooking, teaching, homework with the kids are not items you can drop from your daily to-do list. How about the time you spend checking social media or watching TV? Again, I'm not saying these are bad habits. But they might be the area where you could scale back to find that precious 30 minutes to work on being happy. Only you can decide your priorities. And don't worry, I will address the whole issue of how you regain some space and sanity back into your hectic teaching schedule in an upcoming chapter.

5. Once you have found some time in your schedule, commit to getting to your classroom ten minutes earlier than usual. Be very selfish with this time. Lock the door and turn off the lights if you need to. This time is for you, not your students, parents or co-workers. Take this time to set your intention for the day. Sit quietly and close your eyes and visualize you and your class having a great day. What does that look like, sound like? Connect to the feeling of what that feels like. Feel the quiet satisfaction of when a student makes a breakthrough in learning or the way you feel when the whole class is laughing together at something. Visualize yourself remaining calm and positive even when students are challenging. For the primary grade teachers who likely have a behavior management chart in their room, visualize all of the cards on green or the clips on purple or whatever the physical evidence of a "great" day looks like.

6. It's easy to discount the value of visualization, and connecting to positive feelings of things that you haven't experienced yet. Like my idea of "happy comes first," it can seem a little "woo-woo." But the science behind the positive benefits of visualization has been repeatedly proven. Specific thoughts can stimulate the same areas of the brain as actual actions. In numerous studies, it has been determined that the same areas of the brain light up regardless if someone is simply visualizing firing up certain muscles groups or if they are actually moving them. Athletes attest that an essential part of their training involves visualizing themselves performing at peak levels. So visualization can be a very powerful tool in mental rehearsing and setting a positive expectation for your day.

Make Like A Child and Be Here Now

One of our greatest barriers to experiencing a "happy life" is the idea that "being happy" is a future event. It is the idea that I discussed in the introduction, the notion of "I'll be happy when..." You can fill in the blank for whatever is meaningful for you. Within the context of our teaching I'm guessing the list includes some or all of the following ideas:

I'll be happy when I have...

- better behaved and better-prepared students
- more prep time
- smaller class sizes
- more instructional aides or teacher assistants in the classroom
- less demanding administrators

- more cooperative parents
- more holistic ways to measure student success than standardized tests
- more resources for the classroom
- more respect from students, parents, peers, administrators, the general public, the media...more respect from everyone, basically
- better pay and benefits
- when summer or retirement roll around (if we can make it that far)

You can't delay being happy. The place to be happy is here, and the time to be happy is now. Sure, a week in the Bahamas all expenses paid and no students in sight sounds amazing. But if you move to that beach on a permanent basis, within a couple of months, you might well find that you run into the same obstacles to your happiness that you had when you were living in the burbs and commuting to school every day. The greatest obstacle is your mindset and your habits, not your life circumstances.

My intention in saying this so bluntly is for you to feel empowered and hopeful, not shamed. Having all graduated long before Harvard was offering those classes on Positive Psychology, no one has taught us how to be happy. The idea that much of being happy is a matter of mindset is great news. The even better news is that we spend our day with children, and children are good at being engaged in the present moment. We can learn from them!

Repeated studies show that one of the basic building blocks of a happy overall life experience is the ability to engage in the present moment. There are two essential aspects to this. One is the idea of immersed engagement and "flow state." That is what I will be addressing in this chapter. The other building block is the notion of mindfulness, or quieting our "busy mind." Left to its own devices, the mind will usually obsess on the past or worry about the future. I will address specific habits for quieting the mind in the next chapter, "Brain Breaks for All." Practicing habits related to immersed engagement and mindfulness is important as these habits can improve our happiness and also directly benefit our students.

Let's start with flow state. Pioneered by the work of Mihaly Csikszentmihalyi, (yes, I triple checked that) "flow state" is the state of being deeply engaged in an activity, totally immersed and not thinking about anything else. It's what athletes sometimes call being "in the zone." People often report losing track of time and having heightened focus when they are in a flow state. Being in a flow state can be very relaxing and is the reason why many people can lose themselves in a hobby for hours at a time. While the phrase "flow state" wasn't coined until the 1990s, it is a concept that has long been recognized as being closely aligned with increased feelings of well-being. Even Shakespeare noted,

"Joy's soul lies in the doing."

I find it very easy to get into a flow state when I am using my hands and being creative. I often lose track of time and can spend a whole day quilting, painting or writing. My father once said he felt that people were happier when they had jobs that "produced things." I'm not suggesting we'd all be happier if we had manufacturing jobs, but there is something deeply satisfying in engaging in a hobby that has a physical product as a result.

Unfortunately, one of the stresses involved in being an educator is precisely this lack of "tangible results" to measure our success. We all know that standardized tests aren't a true indicator of what students have learned. But from the outside perspective, what other indicators do we have?

One of the things I loved most about teaching first grade for nine years was that it was easy to witness a significant growth in skills and maturity in the students over the course of the year. All I had to do was save a drawing and a few sentences written on day one of the school year and compare them to similar samples on day 180. The improvement was always significant and it was pretty easy to feel good about everything I had taught them. Or more accurately, what they had learned.

As a quick aside, I am reminded of a non-teacher friend who unintentionally took the wind out of my sails when I was reveling in how much reading progress my first graders were making one year. He said, "Did you really teach them to read, or did you just happen to be there when it happened?" My initial impulse was to invite him to spend a few weeks hanging out in first grade and see how much learning "just happens." But his point was not lost on me; it is true that many times skills develop on their own timetable. It's still a privilege to guide that process and celebrate it when it happens, and it is a lot easier to do in the lower grade levels. As students get older it is harder to see such a dramatic increase in skills across the year. Also, when it comes to things we hope to have taught students outside of the approved curriculum, such as character and life lessons, we have to take a leap of faith. It may well be years until it is evident if our well-intentioned wisdom fell on fertile soil. We all love to share the heartwarming yet fictional story of Teddy Stoddard (come on, you know that one. If not, grab a tissue and Google "Teddy Stoddard story") but in reality, few of us will ever know if we've had a meaningful impact on most of the lives we have touched.

Back to flow state. It would be nice to think we can regularly get into the flow state teaching. Few teachers these days get to spend their day teaching art, music, woodshop or anything that might involve using our hands. Achieving a flow state teaching long division or five-paragraph essays is trickier. But there are two things that I know for sure are "death to flow." These two culprits are multi-tasking and scrambling. To the casual observer, they might look like the same thing, but they are not. Let's look at them a little closer.

As teachers, we pride ourselves in our ability to multi-task. Talking and lecturing, writing on a board or under a document camera, interacting with technology, while simultaneously checking for student understanding and managing behavior is what "teaching" in a classroom looks like. We are adept at walking around the room and talking, redirecting behavior non-verbally as we stand behind students who are chatty or off task. Simultaneously we hand out papers, supplies and bathroom passes and push down on the backs of chairs to keep students from rocking. Skilled teachers are like great orchestra conductors, seamlessly coordinating a thousand moving pieces into one cohesive piece of beautiful learning. So the very act of teaching itself involves multi-tasking, there is no getting around that. The multi-tasking I am referring to that impedes your flow is any attempt at trying to accomplish this delicate balancing act AND still do something else. For example, check your e-mail while students are working independently for a moment. Obviously, your mobile phone shouldn't be out when you are teaching; most campuses have rules about that. But most of us interact with technology all day and use it to teach, so it can be almost automatic to click on your e-mail when you see you have a new message. If students are working in groups for a few minutes, it can be tempting to tackle the pile of papers on your desk that needs attention, correct a few assignments or enter some grades.

One thing I do enjoy about teaching is that for the six hours a day that I do it, it's all-consuming. I find that I am so busy juggling all of the moving parts that I don't have time to think of concerns outside of school, and the day goes very quickly. I often find myself in flow state. I like to be present with my thoughts and my attention in the classroom, with the students 100% of the time. That means if students are working independently or in groups, I circulate, checking in with them. I am the teacher who kneels next to their desk to help them with something or ask probing questions, "Why did you do it like that? How else could you do it?"

I know there is currently a movement in education that strives to decrease teacher involvement, reduce direct instruction and encourage students to work together to solve problems. These are all great objectives that I support. However, we need to be cognizant that the goal for this change is to encourage autonomy in students and have them take more responsibility for their learning, not to free up the teacher's time to do other things. One of the most effective gifts we can give our students is our presence. That means we are engaged with them and available for them. When we ask them questions, we have the patience to wait for and listen to the answers. I know that seems obvious, but it's easy to fall into bad multi-tasking habits when there are so many demands on our time.

So multi-tasking is trying to do anything other than be 100% engaged with your students when you are teaching. Scrambling is something a little different. Scrambling is the result of being underprepared.

Now without doubt, we've all had times when we have had to "wing" our lesson plans. Learning opportunities disguised as "tangents" regularly occur in an engaged classroom. We lovingly call them "teachable moments," even though they take us off topic and down paths we hadn't planned on traveling during that particular lesson. At such times we are required, as talented educators, not to avoid these unexpected wandering roads but to artfully stumble our way through them, often unprepared, confident that we can get to the important learning and then back on the well-trodden path of our lesson plan. That's not the type of "winging it" I'm referring to. I'm referring to the type of scrambling that happens when we are flipping through a teacher's edition to see what's coming up next, or walking around the room looking for supplies as we give instructions. The type of scrambling that comes from not being properly prepared for all of our instruction for the day.

The problem with this scrambling is that it takes us out of flow state and, worse, allows for that tiny moment of unstructured time in the classroom that some students interpret as an invitation to get off task. We are all too aware of this teaching formula:

distracted teacher + off-task students = student behavior issues **

You might be thinking that only an "unprofessional" teacher would show up to class underprepared. Or you might assume that it would be new teachers, unfamiliar with new curriculum and overwhelmed with responsibilities, who would fall into this trap. On the contrary, the teachers who are most likely to just show up with just a general idea of what they are going to teach and "improvise their way through it" (otherwise known as "winging it") are the veteran ones.

It's an easy habit to fall into if you are a teacher who has been teaching the same subject or the same grade level for multiple years. Let's face it, unless you are teaching science or at the college level, the curriculum we wade our way through every year is pretty tried and true. A five paragraph essay is always going to need a thesis statement and follow the formula of main idea and details. Pi is always going to be 3.14, and the sequence of events of any major historical event is essentially going to be unchanged. It's easy to understand that we can get a little complacent (even bored) with the actual subject matter when we have been teaching it for several years. We all know teachers who have taught the same subject or grade in the same room for literally decades. There is a distinct difference between "teaching twenty years," and teaching the same year twenty times. None of us want to have the reputation of being the latter teacher.

One way to stay engaged with the subject matter and increase the likelihood of getting into a flow state is to challenge yourself to teach the material in different ways. First, this will make sure you are prepared, as you will need a specific plan. Additionally, it will encourage creativity on your part.

Research suggests that flow state in children is easiest achieved when they are challenged to their zone of proximal development (not too easy to be bored, not too hard to be frustrated) and when they are engaged in a hands-on activity. We can adopt these same concepts to help us achieve our flow state when teaching.

First, minimize all distractions and multi-tasking by being prepared. Then, challenge ourselves to teach the concepts in a new way, using creativity and a hands-on approach as much as possible. Engaged students are a bi-product of engaged teachers.

Being creative with your teaching is very important, but it can be tricky to do. The first time you teach something, you will find that your Teacher's Edition of the curriculum is your best friend. Your teacher's edition is the culmination of many years of research and the result of close collaboration of top specialists in your particular field. It has been carefully crafted to cover all of the content standards. It likely has more companion editions than can comfortably fit on your shelf or that can be realistically covered in 180 days of instruction. If you are teaching lower grades, it comes with pages of accompanying worksheets to keep your students busy with very little preparation on your behalf. It is an excellent resource, and much of your school district's budget likely went to the purchasing of it. All of this is great. The problem is that, unless you are careful, teacher editions can be stifling from a creativity standpoint.

Depending on how long you have been teaching, you might be aware that there is a pendulum that swings from one extreme to the other with regards to how reading and writing are taught in grade school. At one end of the spectrum is "direct phonics instruction", focusing on specific decoding skills and only using materials that specifically reinforce the phonic element being taught at that time. At the other end of the spectrum is the "whole language approach" where reading is less explicitly taught but acquired through broad exposure to texts and strategies such as using illustrations for contexts clues.

When I began teaching in a first-grade classroom, the pendulum was as far towards direct phonics instruction as it can go. In addition to having been required to spend a week over summer in a class learning specifically how to use the teacher editions, the school was assigned a "coach" from the curriculum publisher. This coach (not so affectionately referred to by the staff as the "Curriculum Police") would show up in the classroom to ensure that we were following the "script" from the teacher's edition verbatim, and that each teacher from that particular grade was at the same place in the curriculum on the same day. For example, we were all expected to be studying Unit One, Week Two, Day Three on the same day. Death to creativity. And also a little demoralizing for a new teacher. It often made me wonder why a profession would require a minimum of five years of higher education if teachers were just going to be given a script to follow like a trained monkey. It also sends a message that there is a lack of confidence in our professional capabilities.

Thankfully, the days of the Curriculum Police have passed. Few professional development budgets these days can accommodate staff training for a whole week during summers and "coaches" milling around. However, the systematic disappearance of teacher autonomy is one of the greatest frustrations for educators in the United States today. I say "in the United States" for two reasons. First, although I attended school in three different countries in Europe, I have never taught there, so I can't speak for their teachers. Second, unless we have all been hoodwinked by Finnish propaganda, some smaller countries seem to be getting the balance right. Here's what I know. Legislation that penalizes schools for poor student performance, as well-intentioned and maybe even necessary as it may have been, has led to an ever-increasing pressure to have students perform well on standardized tests. Coupled with the harsh reality of shrinking operating budgets, many educators have seen the traditionally more "creative" subject areas such as art, music, drama and even GATE (Gifted and Talented Enrichment) eliminated from their campus. We often feel pressured to "teach to the test," spending little or no time on content areas or activities that won't directly impact our students' proficiency in standards included in the year-end tests.

The degree of autonomy that we have in your classrooms will vary greatly on our district policies and our administrator's management style. Some districts merely require teachers to prepare a scope and sequence overview of what we will cover during the year. They will provide the adopted curriculum as a guideline and check in with teachers when test scores arrive. If students are performing, ideally the message should be, "Keep doing what you're doing!" Other districts may require teachers to submit specific lesson plans and then micromanage the process to ensure that the teacher's editions are being followed very closely.

I am currently lucky to work for an administrator who doesn't bat an eyelid when I declare an impromptu Willy Wonka Day. It is now a third-grade tradition that I show up to school dressed as an Oompa Loompa, complete with green hair and white eyebrows and Wonka Bars concealing golden tickets in hand at the end of my Charlie and the Chocolate Factory unit. I consistently find that, as well as having good old fashioned fun, my students produce some of their most creative writing on Willy Wonka Day. It certainly creates positive and meaningful memories for them that remain long after those year-end tests have been taken.

Unfortunately, not every administrator will be supportive of these types of scenarios. However, don't just assume they won't. Have you ever approached your principal with creative ideas and been turned down? Does your administrator know what goes on in your classroom on a day to day, minute to minute basis? I understand that certain district policies are completely beyond our control. But whatever the style or policies of your school district are the fact remains that, as professional educators, the responsibility falls on us to ensure that lesson plans are engaging and as creative as possible. Not just because this facilitates student learning, but because creativity is an important component of our flow state and happiness.

In *The Happiness Hypothesis*, Haidt explains that people achieve the highest amount of job satisfaction when they experience "occupational self-direction" - the flexibility to be creative in their jobs. A 1964 study by sociologists Malvin Kohn and Carmi Schooler showed a direct correlation between the degree of job satisfaction and the degree to which people were allowed freedom in how to approach their work. That's bad news for the Curriculum Police.

Thankfully, technology has made it increasingly easier for teachers to share creative ideas. Thousands of ideas ranging from easy art projects to creative writing prompts can be found on websites such as Pinterest. The internet is full of websites and blogs where creative and passionate teachers share their ideas and lesson plans. Even the quickest search can yield more ideas than you could ever incorporate into your entire school year. Veering away from the prescribed teacher's editions takes time and planning, but there is no need to reinvent the wheel. We are lucky to work in a field where so many practitioners freely share their ideas for the greater good of all. Even if it takes a little extra time up front to infuse variety and creativity into our plans, the payoff in increased passion, engagement and flow makes the time and energy investment well worth it.

For those of you who work with elementary age children, you have an extra advantage in the "get into the flow" department. Your students can be your role models. Young children instinctively know how to be in a flow state. Just look at them playing. They are often totally engaged in what they are doing, with no room for any thoughts about what they just did or what they will be doing later. This is one of the reasons that transitioning between activities can be hard for them. When at play, young children are naturally happy. They are often fully absorbed with whatever they are doing, most of it with the goal of simply having fun and doing what they they like to do. With fewer anxieties about the future and regrets about the past, children live more in the present than adults and are apt to spend less time being goal driven and more time simply engaged in activities because they are fun.

We can learn a lot from children in this area. We have become increasingly conditioned to feel there is no room in the school day for creative play, fun, and silliness. Any time that we can create opportunities for these elements in our lives outside of school can only benefit our teaching in the long run. Selectively incorporating these elements into our classroom even for brief moments is better still.

Recap of this Happiness Mindset Habit:

Recognize that being happy cannot be put off for some future time when circumstances improve. We can only be happy in the present moment. A key component of happiness is the ability to be fully and actively engaged in what we are doing, also known as "flow state." To maximize our flow state potential when teaching we should avoid multi-tasking and also ensure we are adequately prepared for every lesson. Additionally, as the ability to be creative and engage in "occupational self-direction" are critical factors in job satisfaction, we should challenge ourselves to find new and engaging ways to teach the curriculum that is familiar to us. Finally, we can learn a lot from younger students who are more apt to be engaged in the present when they are playing and having fun.

Ways to Practice this Mindset Habit Starting Today:

1. Students value your presence and complete attention. Commit to minimizing distractions when you teach. Put your phone in your desk or your bag. Your kids, your spouse, your family know where you work. If there is a true emergency, they can call the school. When students are working independently or in groups, circulate and engage with them.

2. Gently let it be known on campus how much you value a distraction-free classroom. There is only so much control you have over how many interruptions you have from the school office. However, you can make a significant effort not to disrupt other teachers when they are teaching in the hope that they reciprocate. It's convenient to call another classroom or send a student on an errand to another room while whatever you need or want is on your mind, but try to wait until a break so as not to interrupt anyone else. Hopefully, they will afford you the same courtesy.

3. Challenge yourself to explore new ways to teach at least one period a day this week, or one subject if you teach multiple subjects. As well as looking on the internet or Facebook and Pinterest groups for lesson plans and ideas, dust off some of your professional development binders. No doubt over the years you have been presented with many good ideas that you were excited to try at the time, but never got around to. Focus on activities that are more engaging and creative. Extra credit, if you can make it somehow fun. For example, I am very grateful to whoever posted the School House Rock multiplication songs on Youtube. I often put them on as a filler as we transition from math to the next subject and we have spent many hours in class singing along and laughing. It's always so rewarding to hear students humming the tunes when they work on their math.

4. Appreciate the value of doing things purely for fun. Go to the discount store and load up on anything that takes your fun fancy. Sidewalk chalk, a whoopee cushion, a cheap kite, bubbles, a nerf ball, a hula hoop. Commit to playing for a few minutes each day. Finding time to have fun with your students is best, as even high schoolers get excited for a quick game of "silent ball." If you feel there's no way to incorporate a few minutes of play/fun into your school day, find a way to play at home with your family, your pets or even just by yourself. I often interrupt my evening walk with a quick play on the swings at the park if they're available. It only felt awkward the first few times :)

** Classroom Management

A side note about classroom management. The strategies in this book assume that you already have an effective classroom management plan in place. I firmly believe that being a happy teacher will improve the energy and behavior in your classroom, but it won't be enough to save you if you don't have control of your students. Here is my happy teaching formula. It's a happy loop.

Happy teacher = engaged class = less behavior management issues = happy teacher

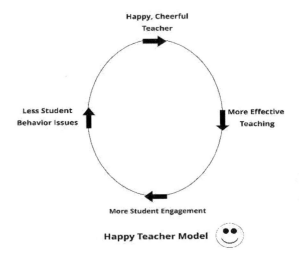

Happy, Cheerful
Teacher

Less Student
Behavior Issues

More Effective
Teaching

More Student Engagement

Happy Teacher Model

It is going to be difficult to create a positive classroom experience for either you or your students if you are engaged in a power struggle and you are unable to calmly and pleasantly keep your class under control. If you feel you could improve your classroom management skills I encourage you to seek support in that area in addition to working on the happy habits in this book. While better energy in class will go a long way to improving student engagement, it will not magically make all problem student behaviors disappear. A solid classroom management plan that you can implement calmly and consistently is a foundational piece of your teaching success. Ensuring you have the best possible skills in this area is one of the best investments in professional development any educator can make. Don't be shy about communicating with your administrator if you feel you need extra training in this area. Controlling students is one of the most stressful aspects of our job, and there are great resources available out there to help you. It's something we have all struggled with to varying degrees. It is your professional responsibility to ask for additional training if you feel you need it.

Brain Breaks for All

"Walk as if you were kissing the ground with your feet."

Thich Nhat Hahn

One of the best tools that we can have in our happiness mindset toolbox is the ability to take a "brain break." A brain break is a short "time out" for your brain, where you calm your mind chatter and connect to the present moment. Left to its own devices, the brain is constantly whirring like an old time movie projector. The movie it's showing comprises 90% of thoughts of the past (regurgitating what has been said or done) or planning, worries and concerns about the future.   A brain break is a way to calm your "mental noise." It's a way to project some blank space on the screen and just connect to the present moment.

As I explored in the last chapter, happiness can only be experienced in the present moment. While it is true you can feel happy when you remember something positive or anticipate an experience that you have positive expectations about, technically you are experiencing the joy in the present moment. That might seem like a philosophical argument, so let's stick to the scientific facts.

The technical term for making a conscious effort to engage in the present moment is called "mindfulness." In spiritual traditions, mindfulness is frequently associated with meditation and the practice of being still and observing your thoughts without judgment.

In recent years, mindfulness meditation has made the transition from a spiritual practice with a deep root in wisdom traditions in the East, to a mainstream medical tool in the West. It is regularly prescribed by medical practitioners to help people manage stress and has been embraced by many top businesses and even schools as a tool to improve physical and mental well-being.

In January 2015, NBC news ran a story about how introducing meditation into four San Francisco high schools had yielded very positive results. Over a four year period, the suspension rate in one high school decreased by 79%, attendance improved, and so did the academic performance. Here's my favorite part of the news story,

"Blocks away at Burton High School, which was once dubbed "Fight School," the results have been similar. Principal Bill Kappenhagen was skeptical at first, as well, and had to wrangle with the problem of when in the school day to grab a half hour for quiet reflection.

"I was like, 'There's no way I'm going to steal time from English instruction or math instruction in order to do that," said Kappenhagen.

Instead, he decided to extend the school day by 30 minutes for meditation time, which resulted in better academic performance and a 75 percent decrease in suspensions. And students say they're more conscious of their actions, calmer and less angry."

https://www.nbcnews.com/nightly-news/san-francisco-schools-transformed-power-meditation-n276301

Right now you might well be feeling like Principal Kappenhagen. You may be "wrangling" with the idea of how on Earth to fit half an hour of "quiet reflection" into your day. I know some days I struggle to get in 15 minutes of silent reading, and that certainly seems like a more essential activity to a school setting. But the good news is that you don't have to find thirty minutes. Recent research has shown that very tangible results can come from short but consistent mindfulness exercises, exercises I am calling Brain Breaks.

Brain Breaks are short practices that can easily be conducted in the classroom that have a foundation in neuroscience. There is nothing "new age" or spiritual about them. You needn't worry about negative reception from administrators and ultra-religious parents as long as you present them as such. The reason to practice them in the classroom is not just to reduce your stress and improve your well- being, but for the direct benefit of the students.

In recent years there has been a surge in neuroscience research around the positive benefits of mindfulness meditation. The benefits of having students practice focusing and paying attention are self-evident. But emerging research is pointing to benefits of increased overall well-being including a reduction in stress and anxiety in children who practice mindfulness exercises, as a well as an increased ability in being able to recognize and manage emotions, increased self-awareness, self-esteem, and empathy. This means students have a better ability to respond to stressful situations appropriately, rather than just react, which is likely a key component in Mr. Kappenhagen's amazing 75% decrease in school suspensions.

As well as social and emotional benefits, academic improvements have also been noted. Mindfulness exercises can help improve working memory and help with executive functioning tasks such as decision making, reasoning and problem-solving.

So while Brain Breaks will have a direct impact on your ability to de-stress and flex your happy muscle, they will also help students increase their focus, their social and emotional well-being in addition to their behavior. What is there not to love? They can easily be introduced into the classroom as activities taking less than 5 minutes. While it does take a little time and patience to teach them, the rewards for everyone are very worth it.

Here are a couple of Brain Break activities that I have successfully used in 3rd grade for quite a few years.

Note - both of these techniques require some explicit front-loading instruction on how to inhale and how to exhale. While we breathe all day automatically, younger students, in particular, may not be aware of the mechanics of breathing. It's a helpful exercise to have students lay on the floor and practice what a complete breath feels like. Students can close their eyes and place one hand on their belly. With a complete inhale they should feel their belly rise. If you feel for some reason you don't have an appropriate environment for students to lay on the ground, they can do it sitting in their seats, but it's not quite as effective.

Starfish Breathing

This activity works as a great "pattern interrupt" to refocus and calm the class when they first come into the room in the morning or when they return from recess. It only takes a few minutes to teach. Once you've taught this technique it only takes two minutes to perform.

The "starfish" is the student's hand with fingers spread out. Instruct students to extend their arm and put their hand, with fingers stretched out, in front of them. With the index finger of their other hand, they are going to trace around the starfish. Starting with the index finger on the wrist at the base of your thumb, guide them to slowly trace around their fingers, inhaling as they go up the finger, and exhale as they go down the fingers. They will end the tracing at the wrist at the base of their pinky. The trick is to trace slowly, and for you to guide them slowly and calmly as you show them, "inhale, exhale, inhale, exhale" etc. If these instructions seem unclear, just Google, "Starfish Breathing" and I'm sure some examples will be there, it's a fairly common technique. It is also sometimes referred to as "Take 5 Breathing" and taught as an anger management technique to youngsters.

Focused Listening

Have students sit at their desks. They should close their eyes. Some students like to put their head on their arms on their desk. Instruct students to inhale deeply, hold the breath for three seconds, then exhale. Repeat. This is just to signal to them that this isn't playing time, but special relaxation time. Instruct students that they are going to relax and listen for one minute. That's all they have to do. They are going to take inventory of the sounds they can hear for one minute, that's all. I challenge them to hear at least five distinct sounds outside the room. At the end of the minute, check in with students as to what sounds they heard. Be sure to debrief in a quiet, calm voice. I am always amazed by what students hear. Clearly, their hearing is better than mine! I am usually limited to the air conditioning unit, sounds on the playground or the room next door. Some students hear the traffic from the road, the passing train.

Helpful hints. One reason I encourage students to listen for sounds outside the room is that it minimizes the temptation for students to make sounds on purpose. Obviously, as with any activity, you need to model the behavior that is appropriate and explicitly teach your expectations of their behavior during the activity. While we all love the class clown and their stress relieving antics, students need to understand that "fake" snoring or tapping under the desk is not appropriate for this type of activity. Even with every best intention in the world, realistically you should still expect a few nervous giggles the first time you try this activity. Don't get discouraged, stick with this. These type of activities, even though they seem simple, really can make a difference to your day and your students' success. Not only will they help you in the short term manage your stress, but over the long term, they can also help you with awareness of your thoughts. I will go deeper into this is another chapter, but for now, recognize that many of these strategies are interconnected.

Another helpful hint is to employ the use of a non-visual cue, such as a symbol, chime, triangle or bell. Much like the entrainment of Pavlov's dog, the repeated use of a sound that is only used when you are about to embark on a Brain Break can be helpful. Over time, students will recognize the sound like an immediate cue that they are about to get calm and centered. Just the sound itself will start to relax them, and you will have to spend less time talking and setting up the activity.

Moving Brain Breaks

Some students have a hard time sitting still. Likely, they are the students who could most benefit from a Brain Break activity. For these students, or for times when you have all been sitting still in the classroom for too long, a moving Brain Break may be preferable. A moving Brain Break is any activity that focuses on connecting the breath and attention with slow, flowing movement.

An excellent moving Brain Break for students of any age would be a simple Tai Chi or Qui Gong exercise of Gathering Chi. Gathering Chi (or Gathering Xi, depending on the origin of the tradition) is a very simple exercise that helps us be aware of our energy and help settle it. To do the exercise, stand up, legs a little wider than hip-width apart. Make sure there is enough room for students to extend their arms without touching anyone or anything. Start with your arms gently by your side. On a deep inhale, float the arms above your head, relaxing the shoulders, and your gaze upwards. On the exhale, turn the palms toward the ground so that the elbows are bent, and float the arms down through the center of your body to waist level, "pushing" the energy down with your hand, and gazing down. Inhale and repeat the upward movement, and exhale, repeat the downward movement. The movements and breath should be slow and flowing. Within a few breaths, if you are focusing, you will feel a tingling of the energy in the palms of your hands, and a calming and "grounding" of your internal energy.

This is a very simple, beautiful and calming exercise, but it can be hard to understand without watching it or experiencing it. There are many YouTube videos on Tai Chi for Kids, or just search Qi Gong or Tai Chi "for beginners." Knowing how to settle your energy is such a valuable skill to have in your tool belt, as well as to teach children. It has taken me longer to explain it than it does to do it, so don't be intimidated to try it.

Guided Brain Breaks

If you are able and interested in investing slightly longer in these types of exercises, there are many great free resources available that you can use to lead you and your students through a guided relaxation experience. They are available for students of all ages and levels. You can easily find videos, mp3s or even use one of the many apps available to stream straight from your phone. Some of the most popular apps such as *Calm, Headspace* and *10% Happier* have free versions that you can check out.

My go-to resource for students in the elementary grades is GoNoodle.com. You may already be aware of this amazing, free website as a lifesaver for indoor PE and rainy day recess. As well as housing some of the most fun and annoyingly "get stuck in your head" movement activities, did you know that GoNoodle.com also has a whole section of mindfulness and relation exercises? They have hundreds of short videos that "activate kids' bodies and brains" and is a well-loved resource for many teachers and classes. If you've never tried it I recommend you take a look at it.

Five Things Exercise

This exercise is just for you. You can practice it when you are inside or outside. I like to practice it when I am outside, walking mindfully across campus. The foundation of this exercise is focusing on your senses. Any time you focus fully on sensations in your body, you give your mind chatter a little break. The practice is very simple. You choose any one of your senses and then focus on finding five sensations simultaneously within that sense for about 30 seconds. For example, focus on hearing five sounds simultaneously. If you choose touch, focus on feeling five sensations in your body - maybe the feeling of the ground under your feet as you walk, the breeze on your face, the raising of your chest as you breathe, the weight of something you are holding, the sensation of your clothes on you or your glasses on your face. You get the idea. When it comes to vision, I like to choose one color and focus on finding five shades of it.

As I said, I particularly like practicing this when walking across campus. Instead of focusing on all the things I need to do when I get to the staff/copy room, or all the things that will happen in a meeting, I take a little presence brain break. In a two minute walk, I can usually run through at least three senses. When I get to the lunch room, I try to completely savor the first bite and see if I can distinguish and find five distinct flavors. Even though these are only tiny increments of brain breaks, the positive effect is cumulative, especially when they become an automatic habit.

These are just an example of easy Brain Breaks that you can realistically start incorporating into your day. I only scratched the surface of the topic, because there are lots of other practical tools that I want to give you in this book. However, I strongly feel there is an increasing need and urgency to incorporate these types of discussions and practices into school curriculum. Technology is changing how we interact with each other and how we spend our time. Twenty years ago there was no need to explicitly teach children how to be comfortable in a state of non-distraction for a few minutes. We are all becoming increasingly addicted to technology, and its alluring feeding of the compulsion to be constantly distracted and stimulated.

I could write an entire book on how essential I think it is for middle and older grade students to learn to sit with their breath and their thoughts for five minutes without the stimulation of talk, music, watching something or fidgeting with a phone. It would be great if we could find a way to incorporate these types of activities into their schedule, even if it's just for five minutes a day. The more pushback and resistance you get from students to the idea, the more likely they could benefit from it.

Luckily, people smarter and more experienced than me already wrote that book. If you are interested in delving deeper into how mindfulness meditation programs have been used successfully in school, and the neuroscience behind them, I highly recommend reading *Happy Teachers Change the World* by Thich Nhat Hanh and Katherine Weare.

Recap of This Happiness Mindset Habit:

A powerful tool for relieving stress is taking Brain Breaks. Incorporating short, simple, Brain Break exercises into your teaching day will not only benefit you, but will help students with focus and improve their social and emotional development.

Ways to Practice this Mindset Habit Starting Today:

1. Commit to introducing one of the Brain Break activities most appropriate to your students starting tomorrow. Just one short activity. Commit to repeating it regularly until it becomes a habit.

2. Spend 10 minutes researching appropriate resources to support you. Grades 5 and lower I wholeheartedly recommend you create a free account at gonoodle.com and look at their offerings. For older grades, spend some time looking at the free versions of some of the most popular guided meditation apps such as *Headspace, Calm, Meditation* and *10% Happier*.

3. Every time you open your door to walk somewhere else on campus, decide on which sense you will focus on and practice the 5 Senses Exercise for one or two minutes.

4. If you want to see quantum changes in your stress level and ability to respond versus react, consider

cultivating a longer mindfulness meditation practice outside of school. Many people are under the misconception that to reap benefits from meditating you need to sit cross-legged for hours, chant, say mantras and follow a spiritual guru. While it's certainly your choice to do that, none of that is necessary to reap the benefits from meditating. There is nothing mystical or mysterious about the positive health benefits of sitting quietly (yes, in a chair is fine) and focusing on your breath, and not being judgmental of yourself when your mind wanders. Meditating, even for as little as 20 minutes a day, can change your brain structures in profoundly positive ways.

5.   There are many great resources out there to help you. One simple way to start is to put an app on your phone. If you want to go deeper and are interested in a non-spiritual approach to meditating, I wrote a short book several years ago titled *Mindfulness Meditation for Beginners - From Zero to Zen in Ten* that you might find helpful.

A Rampage of Gratitude

> "The hardest arithmetic to master is that which enables
> us to count our blessings."
> Eric Hoffer

It has been said that it is impossible to feel depressed and grateful at the same time. In fact, studies have proven that the simple act of feeling and expressing gratitude has a more positive impact on a person's mental health and well-being than almost any other practice.

Much of our ability to naturally feel gratitude comes down to our personality. We all know people who see the glass as "half full," versus those who see it as "half empty." Remember the people Haidt referred to as having won the "cortisol lottery," people who are naturally more optimistic? They tend to find it easier to find things to be grateful for. Your upbringing could also influence this. Maybe you grew up in a family that had regular rituals that incorporated giving thanks, such as "saying grace" before you ate. But again, regardless of your natural set point, you can practice certain habits that will improve the ease with which you find things to feel grateful about.

One of the most powerful habits I have developed over the last 25 years has been that of sharing "three happy thoughts" before I go to sleep. I started this habit years before I knew anything about positive psychology and, unwittingly, I stumbled on a habit that has served my family and me very well. The practice arose from my desire to have a consistent bedtime ritual with my daughter that focused on the positive.

One of the most treasured memories of my childhood was my father giving me a "piggyback ride" up the stairs at night and kneeling next to my bed to say our prayers before I went to sleep. In retrospect, the prayers were simply memorized words that had little meaning to me. I recited them as if they were almost a foreign language. Truthfully, they were pretty somber. The words that I most remembered were, "God bless mama and papa, brother and sister, and everybody who is sick or lonely or unhappy." It wasn't the words themselves that are the cherished memories. It was the safety and security of a consistent nightly ritual with my father that was special. I loved going to sleep wishing happiness and blessings on everyone I knew and loved, and peace for anyone in the world who was suffering.

When the time came for me to start a nightly ritual with my children I resolved to keep things a little more upbeat. My daughter was a very sensitive, inquisitive but anxious child. I couldn't imagine sending her to sleep with similar words and risk hearing "Who's sick? Who's lonely? Who's unhappy?" I opted for reading her a couple of short stories, singing her a song, giving her a back rub and finally, asking her, "Tell me your three favorite things about today." It was a gentle way to end the day and it turned into a treasured ritual. Even though she is now grown and has lived away from home for several years, the last text I often get from her at night is, "Three things?" and we both send each other the three best parts of our day. Most evenings I resolve to run through at least 20 things in my life that I am grateful for as I settle my head down on my pillow. I'm usually fast asleep before I get to number 20. It turns out that old song lyric wasn't wrong, "Count your blessings instead of sheep."

If you have printed out the free supplemental material that accompanies this book, you may recognize the "Three favorite parts of my day" is listed in the daily journal pages. Getting into the habit of looking for and recording the best three parts of your teaching day is a powerful practice. I recommend you put the journal pages on your desk and complete the daily part just before you leave your classroom for the evening. It should only take a couple of minutes. It can become a soothing "closing ritual" for you as you pack up shop for the day, a reflective and positive way to transition from school time to home time. It will also serve to make you think of the things that went right in the day before you return home to your family. That way, when people you love ask you how your day was, you are more likely to respond with something positive.

Another powerful and fun way to incorporate this habit into your day would be to get students involved. You may be familiar with the strategy of "ticket out of the door." In this strategy, students need to hand you a "ticket" with a key learning that they had during the period or day on the way out of the door. The idea is not only to boost accountability in learning, but also to encourage an element of reflection in students before they bolt out of the door. A fun way to end the day is to have the "ticket" be a simple statement about the students' favorite part of the day. Younger students who are unable to write yet can draw a quick picture. The workbook pages have a sample blank ticket template you can use. While you might assume that middle or upper-grade students might use this as an opportunity to be snarky or sarcastic, you might also be pleasantly surprised. I'm often pleased to see what parts of the lesson students connected to. Also, because students are not sharing orally, there is less to gain for the class clown by being outright disrespectful in the hopes of gaining attention or a laugh.

Beyond the "Three favorite things" exercise, there are other powerful ways to cultivate gratitude.

One easy way is to keep a running gratitude journal. I have several completed journals stacked up on my bedside table that I have accumulated over the years. I tend to splurge on journals that feel satisfying to touch - leather-bound, vellum paper. I enjoy sitting with a pen whenever the urge takes me and just spending a few pleasant minutes thinking about things that make me happy and for which I am grateful. In the beginning, the things I was grateful for were very general. I am grateful for my health. I am grateful that my body has produced two perfect children. I am grateful that I awake every morning pain-free. I am grateful for my family. I am grateful that I can read and for all the great books I have enjoyed. I am grateful for libraries. I am grateful for all the positive teachers I had who encouraged me. I am grateful I have a job that I love that challenges and fulfills me.

From family and friends to shelter, healthcare, freedom and democracy, there are literally thousands of things to be grateful for if we have the mindset to look for them. I remember the first days that I worked on my gratitude journal. A few entries would creep out onto the page. But as the days passed and I reread what I had written, I really got into the gratitude mindset. There were days where I felt I was launching on a rampage of appreciation on any topic I set my mind to. Like a muscle that has been exercised, it is a skill I have learned to love. Sometimes when I am sitting on a train, a passenger in the car, yep, even in a staff meeting, I can just pick a topic in my mind and spend five happy minutes on a rampage of appreciation. It floods my body with happy hormones and changes everything about my energy. It is a blissful way to spend a few minutes, but it does require practice like any other skill you are learning.

These rituals are personal. But research has proven that the real magic of gratitude happens when you express appreciation to someone else. Everyone likes to feel appreciated and validated. As pointed out by William Arthur Ward,

"Feeling gratitude and not expressing it is like wrapping a present and not giving it."

So it turns out that one of the most effective strategies is also the easiest to accomplish. Simply thank someone.

In his book *The Happiness Advantage* Sean Achor documents how two simple practices that were introduced to company employees resulted in not only a 30% increase in productivity but also a marked increase in the employees' happiness levels. These two practices were one, list three things a day for which they were grateful (hey, I'd been practicing positive psychology for 25 years without knowing it!), and two, choose one e-mail a day from their inbox and reply to the person with a sincere thank you. That's it. Three blessings and a thank you.

While e-mails are nice, I think there is something even more special about a handwritten thank you note. It tells someone that you took the time and trouble to think of something thoughtful to say. It also has a permanence about it. It is something that you can display and have a visual reminder of someone's gratitude and can also be saved. I have a whole drawer of thank you notes I have received over the years from parents, students, colleagues. They are all in a drawer marked "The Good Stuff." Teaching is an easy career to feel overworked and underappreciated in, and anytime I start to feel that way I like to stick my hand in that drawer and see what happy memory and moments of appreciation I can pull out. The beauty of the thank you note is that it doubles your happiness - it is a morale booster for the person who gives it and the person who receives it.

If you want to take this habit to its fullest potential, you should consider a "gratitude visit" where you hand deliver the note and visit for a while, or maybe take a person out to coffee or lunch to thank them in person. In an extensive study of "well-being", psychologists assigned six therapeutic interventions to the study participants. The intervention that had the greatest long-term effect as far as overall increased well-being was the "gratitude visit."

The great thing about working in a school is we never run out of people to thank! It takes so many people to keep everything running smoothly, and there are many people we can find to express gratitude to without having to go too far. Think about it, from custodians, cafeteria workers, bus drivers, instructional aides, yard duty help, office staff, people who provide care for children before and after school, the list goes on and on. And that's before you even take into account colleagues, volunteers, parents and even past students who make a positive impact on the quality of the day your students have. There is certainly no shortage of people to thank.

Recap of this Happiness Mindset Habit:

The attitude of gratitude is essential to a more positive outlook and life experience. Despite any natural inclinations, gratitude can be cultivated through habit. Incorporate practices into your daily rituals that help you focus on being grateful, and find as many opportunities as you can to share your appreciation with others.

Ways to Practice this Mindset Habit Starting Today:

1. Print out the Positive Mindset Journal pages for the entire six weeks and put them on your desk. Commit to using them! So far in this book, we have covered setting your intention, finding someone to thank and focusing on the three best parts of your day before you go home. The other elements of the journal will be covered as we move forward. The journal is a very helpful reflection tool and gently prompts you to practice these new positive mindset habits. But it only works if you use it.

2. Buy a journal that you are excited about writing in and start listing all of the things for which you are you grateful. There is scientific evidence that writing by hand and journaling (versus typing) serves to positively imprint on the brain, utilizing areas of the brain that are associated with creativity and problem-solving. If you aren't excited by the idea of writing in a journal, you can get an app for your phone. One advantage of an app is that it can provide notification reminders. Also, you can work on it and refer to it whenever you have a spare moment (waiting at the doctor's office for example) without having to feel awkward that people know what you are doing. Even

just keeping a running "note" of gratitude on your phone can work.

3. Schedule some quality "alone" time. Put on your favorite music, grab your favorite drink (tea, wine, beer - no judgment here) and challenge yourself to get a rampage of appreciation going. It can be slow going at first. I suggest that maybe you put a title on the top of a few pages and see if you can come up with 5 -10 positive things you are grateful for in each category to start with. You can add to them over time. Some broad topics to look for treasure in might be:

- family
- friends
- health
- comfort (we all have roofs over our heads, food to eat, transportation)
- education
- work environment (I often remind myself there are people who earn a living working outside doing backbreaking work in harsh conditions. My classroom is clean, warm and safe. I get to choose what I wear. You can start with these ideas if you are having a hard week at work. We all have them from time to time.)

4. Next time you are at the store buy a box of thank you cards. Make a list of at least five people you can thank in the upcoming weeks. One handwritten note a week is a great goal. Remember, these do not need to be

people who are currently interacting with you. There is no statute of limitations on thanking people. One of the most profound and impactful gratitude experiences I had was when I tracked down somebody who had been very kind to me as a teenager. Although I was sure I had thanked them at the time, I wanted them to know, thirty years later, that their kindness and guidance had come at a pivotal time in my life and that the beautiful life I was living now might not have been possible without it. If you trace your own path through history, you will find there were many people along the way who believed in you, positively influenced you or just plain helped you when you needed it. Thank them. Again, there is no statute of limitations on expressing gratitude.

5. Look at your e-mail inbox as a treasure chest. Even though the number of e-mails often seems overwhelming, treat it as a fun challenge to find one e-mail to respond to with an expression of gratitude, along with whatever information is being requested.

6. Start a "ticket out the door" habit with your students. Even if it's just on Fridays, students can share their favorite thing they did or learned that week.

7. Get into the habit of bookending your day with gratitude. Challenge yourself to not get out of bed until you find three things you are grateful for (be mindful not to automatically just recite the same three things every morning) and to fall asleep

counting your blessings. If you have a partner or children or someone you talk to every night before you go to sleep, consider starting a "three happy thoughts" ritual with them.

Reclaim Your Schedule

"Teachers work harder than you, whatever you do."

60 Minutes News Show

That was the opening line of a news segment once featured on 60 Minutes. I'm sorry I can't remember the anchor that said it. But I remember it distinctly because I was new to the profession at the time and I recall thinking, "I didn't know that until I became a teacher." And people don't. I mean, our families start to get clued into the picture pretty quickly. But to be honest, what is expected of us is pretty insane. There is no other way to say it.

Most people think of teachers as being off duty by 3 pm and having "summers off." The reality is that when we are at school, we never stop running. Teaching is the least of it. On the few breaks we have when we don't have yard duty there are phone calls, e-mails, paperwork to be filled out, independent studies to be written, meetings with faculty, meetings with parents, meetings with school psychologists, counselors, nurses, the list goes on and on. Some days it's an accomplishment to have taken a bathroom break and shoved some food in our mouths while we're making copies. And that's before we even get to those two tiny, but impactful, words - "adjunct duties."

When I became a teacher, again, very naively, I thought my job would consist of putting together cute lessons, teaching the cute lessons, and then happily putting smiley faces on papers to "grade" said lessons. I laugh now, and probably you are laughing at me too. But I didn't have any family members who were teachers; I'd never really been up close to anybody who was in education. My children were in kindergarten and second grade, so that was the extent of what I saw come home with them for homework, cute pages with smiley faces. I had no idea of education's little secret that teaching, putting on cute Mother's Days tea parties and having lots of holiday-themed class parties was the least of what their teachers were doing. My first year of teaching I was still completing credential classes one night a week. That was a 60 miles round trip commute. I had two small children at home who still needed help with their homework and school projects. I was learning new curriculum and everything else that goes along with being a first-year teacher (induction classes and project work etc.).

And in addition to all of that, here is a list of additional "adjunct" (synonym for "unpaid") additional duties I was signed up for:

SST (Students Study Team) Coordinator for students from kindergarten through 3rd grade. I actually did that role for five years and at that time the school policy was to only hold SSTs after school.

TOPS Coordinator. Teaching Opportunities for Partners in Science. As our small school did not have a science teacher, I was the coordinator for a program that paired us with local retired scientists who would teach science at our school. It is a fantastic but time-consuming program. As well as on-going work with teachers and the scientist on schedules and lesson plans, it involved multiple trainings during the year in the evening and over summer.

Star Lab Coordinator. For one week a year, I would have every student from kindergarten through 8th grade have an educational experience in a portable planetarium. In addition to maintaining my training in how to run the technology, I needed to set it up and take it down every day, have lesson plans ready for a substitute teacher to teach my class. And, of course, I needed to prepare appropriate astronomy curriculum for each grade coming into Star Lab.

Science Fair and Family Science Night. Have you ever put on a Science Fair? To start with you need to organize facilities, recruit and train judges, create procedures, procure ribbons and certificates. And those are the easy task. More difficult is getting the buy-in of colleagues who feel frustrated they have no more time in their busy day to have students work on science projects and produce beautifully crafted science boards than you do. While very rewarding, it takes a certain type of stamina and personality that can cheerfully deflect criticism and complaints from just about every stakeholder involved - students, teaching colleagues, parents.

The crazy thing about all of this is that these were only the additional duties I had volunteered for. If I were a science teacher, these additional assignments might have made logical sense, but I am a General Education teacher with a Multiple Subject Credential. Wait! I am also fully credentialed to teach a single subject in French and Italian. Those credentials are about as dusty as my NLP Practitioners certification. I might as well have a degree in Dork. Feel free to laugh. But back to the point. These commitments were in addition to other duties that I was contractually mandated to participate in - Open House, Back to School Night, School Board and Parent/Faculty Club Meetings, fundraising events, graduation, yard and dismissal duty. The list goes on and on. Thank goodness that I am not at all athletically inclined and have no experience or interest in sports, or I'm sure I would have been joining all of my colleagues who coach after school, too.

I'm not listing these things to convince you how hard I work. I'm encouraging you to look at your own list because I have no doubt it is similar or even greater in scope. Whether you are in a small rural school like me, or a large urban school, the pressure and expectation that teachers will take on adjunct duties are likely the same. "But it's for the students!" is usually the battle cry that gets us all fired up and guilt-tripped into taking on additional duties. We want students to have a well-rounded education. Because so many of the additional activities such as sports, enrichment, performing arts, music, and band have been cut from standard school curriculum, we assume the responsibility of delivering them ourselves. It's craziness.

Again, we somehow did this to ourselves. This is the result of our teaching culture and allowing ourselves to be victim to creeping normality. Had we been presented with an honest and comprehensive list of all of the things we are expected to do as teachers before we invested time, money and energy getting credentialed, some of us might have hesitated. We start teaching with a class list in one hand and a stack of curriculum in the other, assuming that planning, teaching, and grading would be the bulk of our duties. We assumed incorrectly. Standing in the front of the classroom doing our song and dance to students is just the starting point. Additional duties are incrementally piled on until one day, not too far into our careers, we look at how we are spending our time, and a pretty small percentage seems to be actually engaged in what we love doing - teaching kids. We have somehow created a culture that silently values a teacher who does more, talks more, and volunteers more as a "better teacher." Teachers who volunteer less, leave campus close to dismissal time, and (silly as it sounds) have less student art or projects on their walls, or who rarely speak out in faculty meetings are silently judged as being less committed or somehow "lazy."

The problem with this "more is better" model is that in many, if not most, cases, being over-committed to activities outside your classroom results in us being less effective at the one thing we did sign up to do - teach the students assigned to us. It's hard to be one hundred percent available to our class when we are overly scheduled and overly stressed. With not enough hours in the day, the tendency is to multi-task. From my own experience, I can say that exhaustion and stress lead to resentments building up and a lack of patience with students. And the inevitable occurs - the inverse of my "happy teacher" model from earlier.

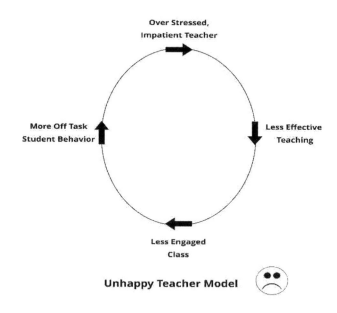

Unhappy Teacher Model

Overstressed, impatient teacher = less engaged class = behavior management issues = frustrated, overstressed teacher.

We all have bad days. There are so many moving parts and personalities in our teaching day that it is inevitable that once in a while we will feel stretched, stressed and a little less patient than we would like. We are human, after all, and we have our limits. We all have any number of elements in our lives outside of the classroom that can be causing a lot of stress. One class period now and then where your students don't get the best of you is normal, and we shouldn't beat ourselves up about it. But being constantly in a state of overwhelm and stress, or impatient and frustrated, is a very big problem that doesn't deliver for either you or your students.

So one of the most significant changes we can make to put the joy and fun back in our classrooms and our lives is to take responsibility for our schedules and our mindset. We need to replace the mindset of "more is better" with a mindset of "less." And not just less commitments, but less "stuff" overall. We need to make space in our schedules and in our physical spaces.

In this chapter, I will explore the idea of less work. I will give you guidance on how to prioritize your adjunct duties in a way that leaves you fulfilled, not depleted. I will also offer suggestions on how to politely set boundaries on your time, as saying "no" to a request can be a challenge for many of us. In the next chapter, I will cover the idea of clearing out some clutter. Physical clutter can weigh us down mentally. Making space in your classroom can be beneficial to both you and your students.

Where to start? There is so much that we need and want to accomplish as teachers, and it often seems like there just aren't enough hours in the day. Is it possible to work less and get more done? I think so. A few years ago I wrote a book on time management and made a compelling argument that focusing on essential tasks, in fact, leads to greater productivity. If you are interested in learning more, you will find the title listed at the beginning of this book. It's the book that starts with *"Stop Procrastinating"*. For the purposes of this mindset, I am not going to talk about time management strategies per se, because there are many other resources available for that. This mindset is not about getting more done; it's about committing to doing less.

Lending our expertise and passion to committees, activities, and clubs that enrich students' lives is a positive thing. Overcommitting and being stretched so thin that we are stressed, exhausted and resentful of constant demands on our time is not.

People tend to over-commit for many reasons. None of these reasons are as "noble" as we think they are, to be honest. Here are some common culprits.

Overvaluing our importance to the project

I used to think my father was very cynical when he used to quip, "Lots of people are convenient, but no one is indispensable." When we think of ourselves as the only person who can do a particular job, we may be overvaluing our contribution. While it feels really good to hear people say, "We could never have down this without you!" the reality is often that the result would have been the same with or without our participation. Someone else would have stepped up to the plate or have been guilt-tripped, or flattered, into the role.

Inability to set firm limits on our time

Many teachers are "pleasers" by nature. Teaching is certainly a helping profession and attracts people who are of an altruistic, service-oriented nature. That doesn't mean we should say "yes" to every request that is made of us. Teachers who have parents texting them at all hours on their phone or sending them daily e-mails and expecting immediate responses are not teachers who are "more committed" than the rest of us, they are teachers who have failed to set polite but firm limits on their time. It may feel uncomfortable to decline requests from colleagues, administrators, and even parents to participate in events and be on committees, but politely but firmly saying "no" is a skill that can and must be acquired. We need to stop being victims. We are as capable of setting limits as anyone in any other profession.

Insecurity of being negatively judged by our peers

When many teachers' go-to response to things not flowing in their classroom the way they want them to is "I'll stay later and take more stuff home with me", the tendency is to judge cheerful, unstressed teachers who only participate in one or two adjunct duties as "slackers." We need to move past the fear of this unfair judgment. I often remind myself that I pursued a career in teaching to help students thrive and grow, not to impress other teachers or administrators. It might seem simplistic, but adopting the mindset of, "What other staff thinks of me is not my business" is a productive first step in reclaiming control over our schedule and our mental energy.

Here are some ways to ensure that our time and energy is spent on our core competency and role - teaching children.

First, limit the number of adjunct duties you commit to. I know that seems easier said than done. You may well have a long list of responsibilities you have committed to through the end of the school year. If that's the case, start a list of items to eliminate next year. When deciding which extracurricular activities to devote your time and talents to, focus on things you are truly passionate about. The criteria for accepting additional assignments should be whether or not they will be fun and rewarding. We should not be accepting assignments simply out of obligation or guilt.

When pairing down my list annually (funny how new commitments silently creep up on you during the year!) the one assignment that I constantly keep is the digital planetarium, Starlab. I love sharing the wonder and excitement of learning about the universe with students of all ages in the planetarium. It's a small miracle to see so many stars, constellations and galaxies. I love when students insist on dragging their entire families to Astronomy Night so that they can experience it. Nothing else I have ever taught has inspired so many gasps and sparked so much curiosity. Having done it every year for over a decade I have all of the curriculum prepared, and in the last few years have scaled it back so that every other grade level participates. That means students get to experience it every other year, and I only need to be out of my classroom for two days. It still requires a lot of work, but to me, it is something I look forward to and an experience I cherish.

Another criteria I use for paring down my list is when in the year the activity takes place. One year I agreed to help with an annual fundraiser. It was a much larger undertaking than I had anticipated and ended up causing me a lot of stress. Even though the most intense work was "only for one month," that month was also the month of Starlab and Astronomy Night. There were weekly meetings I needed to attend that conflicted with a dance class I regularly take outside of school. That dance class is the mid-week fun break that helps keep me balanced. I was irritable and overwhelmed for pretty much the whole six weeks of the project.

I understand there will be duties we need to take on that don't naturally inspire us with ideas of passion and fun. Student Study Teams, fundraisers, School Board Meetings, Curriculum Committees, are all critical areas that need attention outside of our workday. There are certain duties we will be contractually and morally obligated to participate in. We will be more productively involved and cheerfully engaged in these if we limit how many other commitments we voluntarily take on.

Next, get comfortable with declining requests. Teachers are not well known for their fine-tuned negotiation skills. Many of us have a Union that negotiates work conditions and raises for us, so we don't have much experience of being in a place of discomfort with our administrators when it comes to face to face interactions. Many of us end up being overcommitted because we don't comfortably know how to say "no" to people asking for our involvement, especially if we report to them.

We need to find a way to decline requests with a simple but firm, "No, thank you" without feeling the need to justify, explain or come up with a good excuse as to why we are declining. The fact that we don't want to do something should be a good enough reason. I find two strategies helpful here.

One, I have a standard, well-rehearsed answer that I can deliver. Find one that works for you, but mine is usually,

"Thank you for thinking of me, but I'm unable to help you with that at this time. Good luck with the project!"

You get the idea. The three basic elements are - thank you, decline and wish them luck. You can find the words that feel right for you. Note, there is no "I'm sorry" in there. There is no need to apologize.

If you have a hard time saying no to people face to face without squirming, especially if you are taken by surprise by their request, a helpful strategy is to buy yourself some time by saying,

"Let me give that some thought and get back to you."

The intention here is not to blow people off and hope they forgot they asked you, or to avoid them long enough until they find someone else to help them. The intent here really is to give yourself some time and space to consider the request and weigh it against the criteria I set out above. If you decide that it is an opportunity you do not want to pursue you can respond in writing (e-mail or text, as appropriate) with the "thank you, decline, good luck" formula.

Then, set limits with parents. Parents are no different than students in that if you fail to respectfully establish limits with them they will take advantage of you and leave you frustrated and resentful. I remember one year complaining that a particular parent had gotten into the habit of texting me several times some days over ridiculous things. "Can you tell my child to catch the bus today and not wait for pick-up?", "What do we need to wear for the field trip?", "Can you send home another form for sports?" She even texted me in the evening, "What's the homework?", "How do we do the homework?" I was complaining to a colleague who asked, "Who gave her your cell number?" Sheepishly I had to reply that I had. We were on a field trip, and I wanted all of the parents to know how to get ahold of me. That was a legitimate reason, but I had failed to set limits afterward. She began texting me constantly until it just became a bad habit. By the time I was highly irritated by this behavior, I was unsure how to address it without seeming impolite. In the end, I am embarrassed to say that I just waited longer and longer to text her back hoping that she would get the hint. That's neither a professional or productive way to handle such matters.

Setting limits with parents is easily accomplished if we set up a protocol at the beginning of the year and communicate it clearly. Your school may already have a policy buried somewhere in the Student Handbook. The guidelines should be reasonable and presented positively. I always tell parents that the most effective way to get in contact with me is via e-mail. I also explain that because my focus during the day is 100% on teaching their children, I only check e-mails before and after school. All e-mails will be responded to within 24 hours. I provide them with a set time period that I am available for phone calls and meetings. Many parents are unaware that once the final bell goes, most teachers get involved in adjunct duties, meetings and extracurricular activities with students such as tutoring, homework help, coaching. We need to explain to them that requiring an appointment to meet with us before or after school, rather than simply showing up at our door and expecting us to be able to speak to them is not a matter of us being difficult or trying to avoid meeting with them, but a matter of necessity.

Once we define our policy, we need to enforce it consistently. If you make an exception to come running from the copy room to meet a parent who showed up 10 minutes before the morning bell without prior arrangement one time, you will have set a precedent not only with that parent who will likely repeat the behavior but with others who hear about it. We are licensed professionals, and we should start treating ourselves as such. No-one would show up at a doctor's office or a lawyer's office without an appointment and just expect to have 30 minutes of their time. Why do we allow people to do it to us? When a student is out sick and calls the office to have their missing work sent home with a sibling, what is your policy? If you scramble to get it together over your lunch break one time, you have now set a dangerous precedent. I have had parents call and request to pick up a two-week independent study for their child the same or next day. If I have recess yard duty that week, no prep period and a meeting after school, when am I supposed to find the hour or so that it takes to put that together? You know the drill all too well. The details of your situation may differ, but the essential elements are the same. Demands are made of our time and expertise all the time. The fact that on top of an already challenging job, working daily with children, we also have to juggle interactions with parents, administrators, and co-workers means that on any given day, numerous stakeholders will make demands of our time. If we don't have an administration that proactively creates and enforces reasonable guidelines with regards to parent requests, we need to set up and communicate our own and enforce it consistently.

Finally, embrace the idea that you became a teacher to concern yourself with students, not other adults. If you became a teacher for professional respect or for accolades and appreciation from colleagues, you likely have already noticed that you got into the wrong profession. I am not saying you cannot have those things. It certainly is awesome when we are appreciated and respected for our contributions to education.

In ideal circumstances, we collaborate well with colleagues, administrators, and parents. It happens often, and it's a wonderful thing. But it's likely not the reason you became a teacher. You came to work with students and ultimately shape the future by making a difference in their lives. As long as you know you did the very best for your assigned students, that they got the very best of your time, effort and energy then you need to make peace with the rest. Just like I tell my third graders when others criticize you it says very little about you, but reveals a whole lot about their need to be critical. The world has enough martyrs. Most campuses have a group of teachers who constantly overextend themselves and are resentful and complaining that others don't. Leave them to it and don't get dragged into their dysfunction.

Recap of This Happiness Mindset Habit:

Teaching takes an enormous amount of time and energy and we need to be proactive in making sure that we are not overcommitted and overextended. We need to prioritize additional duties that we take on and get more comfortable with respectfully declining requests and setting boundaries on our time.

Ways to Practice this Mindset Habit Starting Today:

1. Make a list of all of the adjunct duties, committees, and leadership roles you have outside of your core function of teaching a classroom of students. Go

through the list and mark which are mandatory or reasonable, and which are voluntary (even if you receive a nominal stipend for them). This second set of "voluntary" duties is where you need to set your priorities.

2. Make a list of activities that you will commit to eliminating from your "voluntary" roster. Some of the items may be commitments that you need to follow through on until the end of the school year. If this is the case, be proactive in communicating with the appropriate parties to let them know in advance that you do not plan on continuing your role next year. The more notice you give people, the less chance that you will be manipulated into continuing because people assumed you would do it and now they don't "have time" to find anyone else.

3. Get a sticky note. Write these three sentences (or similar) on it and stick it prominently on your planner or calendar or somewhere where you will see it as you check your schedule before committing to extra duties.

"Thank you for thinking of me, but I'm unable to help you with that at this time. Good luck with the project!"

"Thanks for thinking of me, but right now my primary focus is dedicating 100% of my time and energy to my classroom and my students. They deserve nothing less."

"Let me look into that and get back to you! Thanks!"

4. Create a set of "Communication Guidelines" for parents and share it with them at the beginning of the year.

Schedule some extra time to spend with your e-mail inbox this week. A cluttered e-mail inbox is overwhelming and unproductive. It's frustrating and time wasting to scroll through three pages of e-mails to find the one you need. If you don't already have file folder categories set up to organize your e-mails, figure out how to do so (plenty of nice people on YouTube will have made videos to show you how) or ask someone to show you. It is very easy and well worth the time investment to set them up. Delete and file e-mails so that you only keep the things in your inbox actionable items that you need to respond to. Take the extra minute to "unsubscribe" from any e-mail lists that you don't need to belong to. Anything you automatically delete without opening is just adding to your mental clutter and overwhelm.

Create Space

When it comes to our classrooms and supplies, many teachers are secret hoarders. We live with constant insecurity that funds to purchase materials will not be available in the future. This uncertainty leads us to hold on to supplies and outdated curriculum longer than we should. Does anyone else have file cabinets filled with odd numbers of "extra" photocopies of handouts that we just can't throw away?

An excess of physical clutter can be mentally draining. Additionally, holding on to things we don't need is also an unproductive mindset in general. It reinforces the idea of scarcity and lack and sets us up to fall victim to the trap of competition for resources.

Education is not a physical commodity. It's not something you can buy at the store. Putting aside arguments of the digital divide and equity in education, if you get down to it, we need very little to teach students to learn.

Every year when I take my third graders to the local pioneer one-room schoolhouse for a reenactment of a day in school in 1876, I am always reminded that the schoolmistress only had her one McGuffie Reader with which to teach all the grades reading, writing, and arithmetic.

When I was a student teacher, I went through a week-long training on how to use literally boxes and boxes of our newly adopted Language Arts curriculum. I'm not saying the curriculum wasn't great, but I do remember joking to a fellow student teacher that somewhere in the world there was a teacher sitting in the dirt with a stick, teaching children to read. They didn't have five boxes of curriculum per grade level. Two years later, that same student teacher and her husband went on a volunteer mission to an orphanage in India. Her husband was helping build a school, and she was teaching. Remembering my comment, she sent me a photo of a bunch of kids sitting in the dirt, smiling profusely with their newly donated supplies of crayons and pencils. She was teaching them to read and write, without even a building to sit in. To this day, I have that photo in my classroom. It reminds me that, even though we should passionately fight for our students to have equitable access to technology and tools to help them compete in today's marketplace, I can't use lack of supplies or resources as an excuse for them not to learn.

Let's be honest. There are things in a classroom that we need. Then there are things that we treasure. Student artwork or projects that we worked on collaboratively would fall into the "treasured" category. The rest of what we have could just be called "stuff," and most of us desperately hold onto way too much of it.

I inherited a classroom that had housed the same teacher for almost three decades. Fifteen plus years later, I am still using the last of the paper that she stockpiled, and also learning that Expos in boxes dry out around the one decade mark. And the problem is not just with supplies. I hate to waste paper. For years I held on to every extra copy that had been made by mistake and dutifully filed it - for next year. In addition, I held onto copies that the previous teacher had made and filed, just in case I could use it. For those of you old enough to remember Ditto or Banda machines, many of those copies were in purple ink. And it's not just supplies, papers, outdated curriculum and half used consumable workbooks. Extra "stuff" can take on many forms, even furniture. Are any of you hoarding extra desks and chairs? When I moved out of that same room a decade later I had to concede that I had held on to a kidney-shaped table I hadn't used in at least five years (although it had been a very convenient place on which to stack up all my "stuff").

We may have legitimate reasons for holding on to stuff. No one likes to be wasteful, and most of us have lived through enough teaching years to know that budgets and spending can often get frozen. If we give up that table or box of Expos now, we might not be in the position to get them back. Some schools have a "use to or lose it" policy regarding class funds that we fundraise which almost incentivizes stockpiling.

The problem with having too much stuff, even if it is shoved away in cupboards and drawers and not visible clutter, is that clutter takes a mental toll. Holding on to stuff that we don't use and don't need is very counterproductive to being relaxed, and allowing new and beautiful things into our lives. It's also stressful to carefully have to navigate around furniture and backpacks in an already crowded classroom. It's frustrating to have to move things around in cupboards and dig through overstuffed drawers and file cabinets to find what you need. When you have to shuffle piles of papers around to create some workable space on your desk the message you are getting sent is that you have too much to do, and you are not in control of it. Visual clutter on the walls, as well as seeing stuff piled up around the room, is distracting to students and can be overwhelming for those who focus best in a structured, orderly environment. If we want to be less stressed and more joyfully productive, we need to make not only space in our schedules but space in our classroom too.

Encouraging you to dedicate precious time to clearing up clutter is not an easy sell. Usually, my classroom starts off the school year in beautiful, orderly fashion. Once the momentum of the school year is going, and piles start accumulating, there are so many more pressing priorities that my tendency is just to ignore it and add it to a list of things I'll "deal with over summer." I'm not suggesting you dedicate weekends to this task and enlist the help of a feng shui specialist. No one has time for that. But I am inviting you to take an honest look at the space that you and your students spend a great portion of your life in. Sit at one of your students' desks and look around. Think about how much time you spend shuffling in drawers and cupboards for things. If it's applicable, look in your craft cupboard. When was the last time you used that half empty bag of jewels and three lonely pompoms? Is it possible that making some more space in your room, your cupboards and on your walls could be beneficial? If the answer is yes, then here are some simple suggestions to help you get started.

Physical Space

Take inventory of your furniture. Are there any extra pieces that you have that could be eliminated? If there are, send an e-mail to colleagues to see if anyone else could use them. Is there a place on campus that extra desks or chairs can be stored? What about traffic patterns in the room? Is it easy to navigate around the room or are you tripping over backpacks? Send an e-mail out to your parent community to see if anyone will volunteer to build cubbies or install hooks inside or outside the classroom for you. A local Boy Scout troop installed hooks outside our primary grade classrooms as part of an Eagle Scout project. Many people belong to church or community groups that are eager to work on school projects once they are aware of them. It doesn't hurt to ask.

Make it a Game

Cleaning out cupboards and drawers is certainly not a preferred task for me. Even though I know it is necessary and beneficial in the long run, it makes me irritable and resentful that I could be doing something more fun. If you are anything like me, if wait until you have a whole afternoon or day to dedicate to this task, you will keep putting it off. So one strategy I find helpful is to chunk the task into smaller units and make it a game. I call it "10 Things in 5 Minutes." I choose a drawer or cupboard and challenge myself to throw out ten things in... you guessed, five minutes. I'm always successful in finding ten things!

Once you've determined which things need to be eliminated, you have to decide what to do with them. Some things need to go in the trash. Other things should be taken to storage rooms or any communal place on campus that people who might need it can get it from. Don't dump stuff in the staff room and leave it there. If no one has claimed it after a few days, then set up a donation pile somewhere on campus. If you are not interested in taking donations to the appropriate place, send out an e-mail request to your community. Someone will do it. Most books and craft supplies would be happily received by after school programs, or can just be sent home with students. Remember all of those odd copies in your file cabinets? Make a "scratch paper" stack on a shelf and students will tear through it quicker than you can keep it stocked. In my class, we would never dream of using "new" paper to figure out math computations or for graphic organizers when planning writing.

Start the Year with Blank Walls

I believe that, especially in the younger grades, students should have a colorful and cheerful classroom environment. My third-grade class has a "Wild About Learning" jungle theme with animal print borders and accents. But when students start off the year, those borders surround pretty blank walls. Throughout the year, I do add things to the walls. There is an art gallery for student work that changes seasonally. However, for the most part, the "content" rich information that I put up the students have either helped me create or watched me create. I use a lot of the Project GLAD™ (Guided Language Acquisition Design) instructional strategies, many of which focus on students' involvement with input when creating charts. There are no pre-printed posters that I have purchased. I find students have no "buy in" to pre-printed posters, especially if they are already on the walls when they start the year. It all fades into background "noise" with little meaning to them other than clutter on the walls.

In upper-grade classes, depending on your grade, there will be a need for scientific data perhaps, or math formulas. But I would encourage you to start off the year as a blank canvas and add these elements as you discuss them.

In recent years, safety guidelines from the fire department have mandated that no more than 50% of the wall space in California be covered, and bi-annual inspections help keep us on track with that. Even if you're not in California, 50% of your wall covered is plenty. Being minimalist in this area helps students pay more attention to what you do consider important enough to be on the walls. It also helps set the tone that the classroom is neat, organized and a professional place where learning occurs.

Here's one final tip on physical clutter. Consider curtains for the bookshelves reserved for your personal use, not ones students need to access. To eliminate visual clutter, I made simple curtains that attach with Velcro to cover the front of bookshelves behind my desk. Even if I have piles of papers and odds and ends on the shelves instead of on my desk, it looks neat and organized. And the fabric, of course, is fire retardant zebra print. Because in third grade we are "wild about learning." My classroom is themed, functional and cute - that's what we call "Pinterest worthy!"

Recap of this Happiness Mindset Habit:

An excess of physical clutter can be mentally draining. Additionally, holding on to things we don't need is also an unproductive mindset in general. It reinforces the idea of scarcity and lack and sets us up to fall victim to the trap of competition for resources. From drawers to walls to furniture - spend some time clearing out extra "stuff" from your classroom.

Ways to Practice this Mindset Habit Starting Today:

1. This is pretty easy. Take an honest inventory of how much stuff you have in your rooms and the physical environment we provide for our students. Make a commitment and a plan to clear out the clutter.

2. Challenge yourself to play the "Ten Things in Five Minutes" game every day for the next two weeks and see how easy it is to transform your clutter into calm.

Remember to include your walls when taking inventory of where you scale back.

Get Connected

"No significant learning can occur without a significant relationship."

James Comer

Studies over the last 25 years have consistently shown that the happiest people are those who feel the most "connected" with social relationships as well as connected to "something greater than themselves." This is good news for teachers.

First, as I have already mentioned, teaching is a "noble" profession. Many view it as a vocation or calling, more than a "job." Let's face it; it's unlikely that you became a teacher for money and acclaim. There are certainly easier ways to earn money, and much of our acclaim comes in the form of hand-scribbled notes from kids. So I am assuming that the second part of the happiness formula in this chapter has already been achieved for you: connection to something than greater than yourself. Teaching is a profession that has the potential to change the future. A free and equitable education is the foundation of all civilized societies and, as such, few professions are as critical, influential, and potentially rewarding as teaching. What we do matters. Even though we might not feel the burning passion of being "connected to something greater than ourselves" every time we are grading a stack of papers or interacting with a difficult parent, teaching has, by its very nature, the potential to fulfill this critical ingredient to our happiness. It has value and connects us to the common good.

Second, regarding social connectedness. Our school day provides us with plenty of opportunities for quality social connectedness. I am emphasizing "quality," in that it allows for social connectedness in the real world, with real people, as opposed to virtual interactions via social media. We all know people who have 700 Facebook friends but who feel socially isolated and have no one to go out with on the weekend. This is not to say that advances in technology have not been helpful when it comes to long-distance social relations. As someone who has lived away from most of my family my entire adult life, I can attest that technologies such as e-mail, Facebook, and video chatting have made a positive impact on my ability to connect with family members overseas. However, research is pointing more and more to the fact that while technology has had a positive impact on helping people maintain long distance relationships, it has had damaging effects on people's relationships with family and friends that immediately surround them. You only have to go as far as a local coffee shop or restaurant to observe people interacting with their phones instead of each other to know this is true.

But let's turn our attention back to school. As teachers, we connect with people all day, every day. We interact with students, fellow teachers, support staff and a large community of parents, grandparents and other stakeholders. The potential for robust and meaningful social relations is abundant.

Now I am not suggesting that we need to be "buddies" with our students. We need to maintain boundaries of respect and professionalism. Teachers are responsible for providing students with an environment where they feel safe, respected, and valued. We have an obligation to be positive and cheerful when around them. Again, we're human. There will be the occasional time when you are in survival mode and trying hard not to look at the clock to see how much longer until the period or your teaching day is over. But it should be the occasional time, not the norm.

A recurring theme in this book is that students learn better and behave better for teachers they like. So, if we want to relieve stress and make our day go smoother, it is beneficial for us to have good relationships with our students. But moving beyond just having a smoother day, I have found that the most magical moments, the most fun, and the most synergy and learning have happened with groups of students that I've had relationships with. Overall, I have a lot more fun with my own students than I do with other classes because we know and like and respect each other; we're connected.

How can we invest in social relationships with our students while maintaining appropriate boundaries?

My experience teaching younger students has been that students naturally like their teacher and want to please them. Most elementary school teachers have more than enough poorly spelled but well-intentioned love notes and drawings from students pinned to their walls to pose a fire hazard. That's the "good stuff", for sure. Connecting with lower grade students really just boils down to finding out what interests them and finding time to talk about that with them. Younger students tend to value one on one time with the teacher, and so then the challenge becomes to try to create as many moments for that as possible. I once heard someone describe their experience teaching second grade as being similar to "being pecked to death by ducks." You know the drill, younger students tend to be very insistent in gaining your attention. On the days when you notice that a particular student seems out of sorts, distracted, or quieter than usual, it's challenging to find time and privacy to check in with them and see what's bothering them. Here are some easy ways to connect with lower grade students:

Get involved in what you are asking them to do. If they are singing a song or dancing - do it with them. Nothing makes my students giggle more than me joining in rainy day recess with them when we do Just Dance or pick activities off gonoodle.com. If you are working on an art project, sit at the table and make the project, too. Whenever I can, I like to have two or three students at a small table with me just working on a project of some kind. Small talk often happens when students are busy with a low key, fun activity.

Interact with them at lunch or breakfast. First, students get a kick out of you standing in line with them, eating with them and cleaning up afterward. Talk to them naturally, there's no need to ask probing questions. I once had a third-grade student whose parents were going through a divorce. It was a difficult time for this student, and I made it a point to have breakfast with her once a week for a couple of months. Ten minutes a week isn't too much to dedicate to a student who is going through a rough patch.

Leave your door open one day a week before school if possible. I try to do so on Mondays. Often students have issues they need to "decompress" about after the weekend. Even though before school may be the only precious minutes of prep time that you have, you will find that the time investment is well worth it if it means students can get straight down to business when the bell rings. Students can be especially hard to settle on Monday mornings if they are still processing personal issues that happened over the weekend.

Find any way you can to have downtime with them. Raising my children taught me that meaningful moments, connections, and discussions rarely happen when "scheduled." You can call a family meeting to discuss things, but what's really on their mind will more likely randomly come up when you are driving them somewhere or just spending time together. You can't schedule "connect with kids" in your planner. You have to put in the time.

Connecting with middle and upper-grade students can be more challenging. Often, the energy that a second grader used to put in to making a love note for their teacher, a sixth-grade student will more likely put into passing a snarky note around the class. Energy is put into avoiding the teacher's attention and attempts to be "buddy" with them are inappropriate and more likely to cause them to cringe. Not always, but enough of the time to make it a little more challenging to connect. The middle-grade years can be very stressful for many students. These are the years that peer pressure and bullying are most likely to occur. Middle school is typically a transitional time in adolescence when students are trying to figure out their identity. Add to this mix some hormones, and it becomes clear why this can be a difficult time for many students. Anyone who has ever worked with or raised teenagers knows that even though students this age can be difficult to be around, it is at this time in their schooling that they need positive role models. And the positive role model for many of them comes in the form of their teacher.

While it can be more challenging to achieve, the strategy is the same. It boils down to creating opportunities for downtime with students.

Here's an example. Before I was fully credentialed, I was a substitute teacher for several months. One day I was called to a seventh-grade class. At lunchtime, there were about 30 students at the door looking for the regular teacher. I thought maybe I had misunderstood the schedule. When I asked if they were expecting class, they replied, "No, we eat our lunch with Mr. Smith and watch *Star Wars*." Turns out only about half of the students were even his. There were some eighth graders who had been his students the previous years, some seventh graders from another class, some sixth graders who "hoped to have him next year." I asked them if they wanted me to figure out how to put on the movie and they said, "That's OK, it's not really about the movie."

The following week I was called back to the same school, but for a different teacher. When lunch came, I wandered over to Mr. Smith's room to introduce myself to him. I secretly wanted to see what kind of teacher would want to repeatedly watch *Star Wars* during their lunch. I have to say, what I witnessed when I went in the room was not at all what I was expecting. Students were sitting around eating; some were talking quietly. Mr. Smith was at his desk eating a sandwich; one student was showing him work from another class that he wanted advice on. Other students sat around him chatting. Everyone was relaxed and hanging out. As I looked around the room, I recognized a couple of students who I had taught the previous week. One, in particular, had stood out as being a little bit of an "outsider." It's hard to say why exactly, he just had a very awkward way about him, had a very high voice, and he was dressed more like an elementary student than a middle schooler. He looked like an easy target for bullies. As I looked around the room, there did seem more than a few students who seemed that they might have a harder time fitting into traditional middle school cliques. At the end of the day, I went back to talk to Mr. Smith. I wanted to tell him, although I'm sure he already knew, how disappointed they students were the day he wasn't there. He just smiled and said that he had started the practice a few years before when a couple of his students complained about having no one to sit with at lunch and now it had grown into a tradition and students expected it. He said that they cycle through all three of the *Star Wars* movies. To which he added, "It's not really about the movie." You get the point.

One strategy that I have seen used successfully with students old enough to write is sending home a low key assignment that is to complete the sentence, "One thing I wish my teacher knew about me is …" It's one way to get to know more about your students, although I feel that doing it in a more organic, less contrived manner is preferable.

A quick note here about setting appropriate boundaries. If we ask probing personal questions, we should be prepared to take on the answers. We are all aware of what are responsibilities are as mandated reporters. I tend not to pose probing, personal questions. I feel that positioning myself as a responsible, respectful and trusted adult in a student's life is enough. I like to think I present myself and my concern about students in a way that would lead them to be comfortable confiding in me if they ever had a serious issue. That has certainly been my experience. But it is important for our stress levels and mental health to set appropriate boundaries when it comes to students' personal problems. Once we have taken the appropriate steps to refer them to the resources they need and, if appropriate, have gotten outside agencies involved, we need to find a way to leave the issue at school. It's not helpful to fret at home or get overly involved in trying to meet every students' needs. It's appropriate to keep extra snacks in your drawer for a student whom you know comes to school every day hungry. It's well documented that a student who is hungry is not going to learn. It's not appropriate to buy students clothes, shoes, an alarm clock, glasses, or whatever else they need. I'm not saying I haven't done so plenty of times in the past, but doing so on a continual basis is a recipe for teacher burnout and a slow building resentment against other adults in the student's life who should be taking care of such things. As my family told me when I started teaching, "We understand that your heart is big enough for all of your students, but our house isn't!"

Let me sum this up quickly about students. We're teachers. We will only be truly effective if we connect with students. Children are no different than adults in the respect that they want to be noticed and validated. Whether we say it explicitly or not, what students need to feel from us is, "I see you. You matter."

Our ability to form meaningful social connections goes well beyond just students. Schools form one large community of parents, administrators, teachers and support staff, volunteers, coaches all working towards the same goal. Over the years, some of the deepest and most lasting connections I have made have been with parents, especially if they volunteered a lot of their time to the school or if I had several of their children in my class throughout the years.

More recent research in happiness has found that merely having a multitude of social connections doesn't automatically affect us positively. Again, we all know the person with 700 Facebook friends and no one to hang out with. It's the act of investing in those connections that reaps the rewards. Investing time and energy in meaningful ways, that benefits others, has the potential to release the "bonding" hormone oxytocin and produce physical and emotional benefits. Being kind is good for you.

Over the years, there has been growing support for a Random Acts of Kindness movement. Some elementary schools actively promote random acts of kindness as school culture and hand out "RAK" tickets to students when they catch them being kind to other students. Character Counts is also a popular program in many US schools and has a "Caring" component. Creating a school climate that minimizes bullying and promotes kindness is important. But as far as our happiness goes, scientists are finding that it's not random acts of kindness that are boosting our bliss, but intentional ones.

So with this in mind, the goal then is not merely to connect with students, but to champion them. Don't simply chat with parents and co-workers, engage in intentional acts that show appreciation of them.

Some of the ideas I mentioned before such as eating with a student who is going through a difficult time, keeping snacks in your drawer, creating a safe place for non-popular students during lunch all fall into the category of intentional acts of kindness. The beautiful thing about them is that they benefit the recipient, but they also directly benefit our happiness.

There are so many ways that we can create opportunities for intentional acts of kindness. They needn't cost money, and they needn't take a lot of time. They take thoughtfulness and a willing heart. Some people believe that the extra "secret sauce" to this mindset is doing nice things for people and not telling anyone about it. I'm not sure that there's a need to be super secretive about it, but I think the point is to do kind things because you want to share kindness, not for bragging rights or to draw positive attention to yourself. Here are a few ideas to get you started:

Students

Write the students a note about what you appreciate about them, or complimenting them on something they worked very hard on and hand it to them on the way out of the door.

Choose a student to champion all week. Go out of your way to catch them doing something good, take a little extra time to build them up or to try and connect with them. Give them extra responsibilities in class, if that's something you think they would enjoy. Remember, it's not always the students who are obviously lacking in resources or support at home who need championing.

If your school has a Buddy Bench, keep an eye on it at recess and see if any students need a buddy. If you work at an elementary school and you don't have a Buddy Bench, it would be an awesome project for you to work with your student body, other staff, or parents to fundraise and organize procuring at least one for your campus. It would also be a beautiful act of kindness to dedicate the bench to an unsung hero of your school community. For those of you who haven't experienced one, a Buddy Bench is a designated bench on campus that students can sit on if they have no one to play with. The idea is that if a student sees someone sitting on the bench alone, they will invite them to play.

Make "day maker" phone calls a regular part of your routine. A "day maker" call is when you call a parent or guardian and make their day by saying something positive about their child. As well as spreading happiness, these types of calls also foster goodwill and can work to a teacher's advantage. If you have to contact a parent at another time for less than great reasons, parents will already have had a positive experience with you and tend to be more responsive and less likely to believe their child if they say you don't like them or are "picking" on them. One of the great things about technology these days is that you can easily send a "day maker" e-mail or text. Many teachers prefer this as it is quicker to accomplish and doesn't come with the concern that the parent might keep you on the phone longer than you had planned. Day maker notes are best of all, as they provide a keepsake.

Co-Workers and Other Adults on Campus

Pick up an extra cup of coffee or bagel on the way to work for a co-worker.

Offer to cover a co-worker's recess or after school duty on a day that they aren't feeling so well or are having a tough day. If you share the same students, offer them your prep period once in a while just to be kind.

Remember that it can be very overwhelming for substitute teachers and aides to be on a new campus where they don't know the rules, routines, the staff or the students. Be aware of new faces on campus who would appreciate someone offering to show them around, let them know where they could get some water or put food in a fridge, or even just to have someone to chat with them at lunch. Sometimes even the adults could do with a Buddy Bench.

Take advantage of how much students like to be helpful, and see if there are any small things that your class can do to make someone else's day easier. Maybe spend your recess or PE period picking up trash, or helping out in the cafeteria if that's appropriate.

These are just a few ideas. There are so many small acts of kindness that you can accomplish with relatively little effort. They may seem small to you, but they might make a huge difference in someone else's day.

Here's an example of something that happened to me years ago when I was teaching first grade. Every time it was a student's birthday, the class would sing to them. As my family mostly lives overseas, sometimes I would have my whole class call my mom and dad on their birthday. It thrilled my parents, who never got to see me on their birthday. And it thrilled my class and gave me the opportunity to teach them about time zone differences. Anyway, one day a little girl said, "It's my dad's birthday, can we call him?" There was a tiny part of me who didn't want to set a precedent of calling every parent (I was surprised that in nine years she was the only student who has asked) but there was a larger part of me who wanted to accommodate a sweet child who rarely asked for anything. Anyway, we called her dad, and I was mildly mortified that I had forgotten it was barely 8:30 AM, and we had obviously woken him up. Clearly, he wasn't the parent who got her to school. No worries, he was very gracious about it, and I soon forgot all about it. Well, fast forward five years, and I was attending our annual school fundraiser. This student's grandma (mom of the sleepy dad) was a well-loved volunteer and member of our community. Her children and her grandchildren had attended our school. Unfortunately, she had not been on campus for a while as she was receiving treatment for cancer and had also fallen and broken her back. When I saw her, I rushed up to her wheelchair to hug her. As she hugged me, she told me, "You know I never thanked you for your kindness to James. He was going through a really tough time personally and at work, and he said that your phone call on his birthday made him so happy and was a good luck charm because later that day he found out he wasn't losing his job." It struck me that such a small act of kindness that I had quickly forgotten about had made such a significant impact on someone else's life. And that even though this lovely woman had so many other things on her mind, she too had been very kind at that moment to take time to thank me.

Recap of this Happiness Mindset Habit:

A key component in happiness is feeling connected to other people and connected to a cause greater than ourselves. Teaching provides us with ample opportunities to practice both of these mindsets. Anything that we can do to connect with students and adults and any opportunities we can create to practice intentional acts of kindness will not only benefit others but also boost our happiness. It's a win-win situation.

Ways to Practice this Mindset Habit Starting Today:

1. Take some time to reflect on your own life. Think about acts of kindness that positively impacted your life along the way. Think especially of when you were in school. What did teachers do or say that had a lasting effect on you? If there is anyone on that list that you can track down, take the time to thank them. If you don't know the person or how to track them down, you can write them a thank you note anyway in your gratitude journal.

2. Think about your students and co-workers. Decide on at least five intentional acts of kindness you can do in the next month. Sometimes getting started is the hardest part. You will probably find that once you start practicing acts of kindness, the momentum will pick up and new ideas will come to you easily.

3. If you have never seen it, watch Rita Pierson's TED Talk, *Every Child Needs a Champion*. It is only 14 minutes long, but it is a beautiful testament not only to championing children but to the incredible power of setting positive and high expectations for students. Click here, or if you are not reading a digital copy of this book, you can simply Google "Rita Pierson TED Talk."

"We cannot always do great things. But we can do small things with great love."

Mother Teresa

Focus on What You Want

"Your mind is the most fertile soil in the universe. Mind what you plant in it."

Unknown

The quote above has been posted on the front of my desk for over 15 years. Have my students noticed it and found it meaningful? Probably not, especially not the first graders. The quote is there for my benefit, not theirs. It is there to remind me of this next mindset habit which is one that has the greatest potential to transform not only your teaching, but the overall quality of your life experience. If you are successful in mastering this one habit, you will experience a quantum leap in all areas of your life. That may sound like an exaggeration, but it is true. If you commit to trying only one strategy in this book, this one will yield the most significant pay-off for you.

What is this big secret mindset? It's less of a secret and more common sense. It's simple, but it's not easy. The mindset habit is this - focus on what you want.

Now in a classroom setting, you may think that you are well practiced on focusing on the behavior you want. Especially in the elementary grades many of us have been taught that it is much more effective (and pleasant) to praise the students who are on task and doing what we do want, than nag and reprimand students who are not. I hear myself many times a day commenting, "I love the way Jessica has her book open to the correct page already!" It's more fun to see students scramble to get some teacher recognition than it is to complain that students are taking too long to get ready. But this mindset isn't so much about focusing on the behavior you want in others. It's on learning to focus your attention on positive possibilities and positive outcomes.

We live in a culture that is chronically focused on the negative. Researchers have calculated that the average person has between 40,000 - 60,000 thoughts in a day and that for most people approximately 70 - 80 % of those thoughts tend to be negatively focused (thinking about things we don't want to experience or to happen). You might remember the term "negativity bias" from Psychology 101. Negativity bias is the demonstrated phenomenon that even if they are of the same intensity, emotions that are negative have a greater effect on our brains than emotions that are positive. Add to this scenario the research that indicates that as much of 98% of our thoughts today are pretty much the same as the thoughts we had yesterday, and you can see that we really have our work cut out for us to carve new positive neural pathways in our brain. Those old negative pathways are deeply worn trenches and comfortable habits for us. So again, this positive mindset of focusing on what you want is simple, but not so easy.

Why are we so focused on the negative? Anthropologists will point out that believing that the world is a dangerous place and being on high alert for danger served a vital function in the survival our species. Focusing on the negative kept us alive. Now that very few of us have to be on the lookout for tigers while we are hunting for dinner, it keeps us stressed and unhappy. Focusing on what we don't want leads to negative emotions such as:

- sadness for the past
- anxiety for the future
- guilt
- grief
- restlessness
- resentment
- frustration
- disappointment
- inadequacy
- hopelessness

Focusing on what we do want is more likely to result in positive emotions such as:

- joy
- awe
- gratitude
- appreciation/forgiveness
- compassion
- optimism
- serenity/peace
- overall wellbeing

Obviously, if our goal is to feel positive emotions, we are going to have to make a conscious effort to focus our thoughts in a positive manner. That's the whole point of this book. The other habits that I have presented such as recalling the best parts of our day, writing down things for which we are grateful, creating opportunities for intentional acts of kindness, focusing on having fun and connecting with others, these are all strategies to focus our minds in a positive way. Considering that, left to our own devices, our minds will wander down the well-trodden negative neural grooves, and the fact that negative thoughts will affect us more than the positive ones, we begin to understand that if we truly want to "flip" that positive switch, we will need to work these habits daily.

Earlier, I suggested that a "happier life" is essentially made of a life with a string of happy moments strung together. Here I am suggesting that we need to be "Joy Detectives" and train ourselves to the mindset of purposely looking for joyful moments. Once we find them, we need to focus on them so that they become entrained in our mind. Our brains have a natural tendency to hold onto the bad stuff (like Velcro) and let the good stuff roll off us (like Teflon). In order to be happier, we need to flip that. We need to Velcro the good stuff, and Teflon the bad stuff. Simple. Not easy.

Before I talk more "theory", here are a couple of practical activities we can start practicing daily.

Become a Joy Detective

First, we can make an internal game of being a "Joy Detective." I usually challenge myself to find "five things I like" any time I leave my classroom. I hang my classroom keys next to the door. Whenever I pick them up to leave the room it's my cue to remind myself, "Between here and the staff room I will look for five things that I like, and I will find them." What kind of things? Well, anything that pleases me. It could be observing a bird, blossoms on a tree, the sound of students or adults laughing. It could be that I notice a student skipping, students smiling, students playing. It could be a physical sensation, such as the sun on my face or delight of fresh air after being inside for a while. It could be something as simple as liking something a student is wearing and giving them a compliment about it. This might leak into "creepy" or inappropriate territory for older students, but little kids love if you notice their t-shirt or sneakers or backpack. When I walk from my car to my classroom in the morning, I set the same intention. "Between here and the classroom I will look for five things that make me happy, and I will find them." It's a great way to start the day on a positive note.

126

Another easy strategy is to pick one happy experience and focus completely on it for two minutes. It can be something that has happened in your day or an experience that you remember. Take a piece of paper and write down as many specific details about that memory that you can. Where were you? Run through the senses and write down as much as you can remember about what you could hear, see, taste, smell, and feel. Try and exhaust every detail. Then close your eyes and see if you can evoke the feeling of well-being that you experienced until it is palpable in your body. Ideally, you should feel yourself relax, maybe even smile. When you get good at this, you will be able to synthesize your own happiness and stimulate your body to produce cortisol. Therapists used to tell people who were stressed: "Go to your happy place." I am taking it further and saying that to be truly beneficial and "Velcro" the moment, to stimulate new neural pathways, you need to go to your happy experience. Science says writing is an important component of this exercise as it stimulates specific regions of the brain. But if you can't get to paper, even immersing yourself in this memory as specifically and as often as you are able, can have a very specific positive effect.

Change the Channel

Now these strategies seem easy enough. However, you may also remember from basic psychology classes the concept that, "First come the thoughts, then come the feeling, then come the actions." This is the idea that we behave certain ways because we feel a certain way. And we feel a certain way because of what we are thinking. This would be simple enough if it were not for the fact that up to 95% of our brains activity is subconscious, meaning that it happens beyond our conscious awareness. Much of this is taken up by body functions. We breathe automatically, our heart beats by itself, we produce enzymes that digest food, and we have to give little thought to what muscles groups are involved when we move, talk or eat. Many people think that our feelings happen automatically too, depending on external circumstances and what is happening around them. This is incorrect. Emotional feelings are not a result of your circumstances; they are a result of your thought patterns. The problem here is, most of our thoughts are running on autopilot, and so we are unaware that they are negative. We DO have a choice about what we think and feel. But the first step is becoming aware of our feelings because with awareness comes choice.

How can we become aware of our thoughts? Well, developing a mindfulness or meditation practice will certainly help with that over time. But the easier and quicker way to know what we're thinking is to use our feelings as clues. For example, if we are irritable and frustrated, chances are we are having negative thoughts. "Why doesn't that kid ever listen? How many times do I need to repeat myself? Why do I always get the tough kids? How many days left until summer?" The chances are that instead of being a Joy Detective, we are practicing being a Problem Detective. We have conditioned ourselves to be on high alert, waiting for our "problem" students to start acting up. Even when they are on task, we find it hard to relax, waiting for what we have convinced ourselves will be an inevitable incident to occur. Our decisions, actions, feelings, and behaviors are all the result, and clues, to what we are thinking. If we're laughing and playful, chances are we're thinking happy thoughts. If we're crabby and yelling, we're not. We don't need research to tell us that. But where neuroscience can help us is in telling how to change that.

One of the basic practices of Neuro-Linguistic Programming is working with "pattern interrupts." When you find yourself engaged in a routine pattern of negative thinking, interrupt the pattern with a behavior that has nothing to do with what you are thinking about. A classic pattern interrupt technique is to wear an elastic band (ladies, a hair tie works great!) around your wrist. When you find yourself in a negative "groove" in class, ping the elastic band. Another effective pattern interrupt technique can be a simple, "Stop, Breathe, Ask" exercise. When you recognize that you are heading down the overwhelm, irritated, negative road simply stop what you are doing, take a deep breath, and ask yourself what I call an "essential question." Here are some examples of questions I ask myself,

"Is this what I want to be feeling right now?"

"Are these thoughts moving me towards my goals or away?"

"Are these thoughts facts or stories?"

This last question can be especially helpful when your mind is racing and creating future scenarios that may or may not materialize, or when trying to interpret the motivation behind what other people have said or done to you. The reality is that we never really know what's going on with other people. Many of the stories that we make up in our head of perceived disrespect and insults that others have wronged us with are just that, stories. They may realistically have more to do with us being in "victim" mode than other people's true intentions. I encourage you to define an "essential question" that resonates with you and write the letters "S, B, A" on small stick notes. Stick them on your desk, computer, mirror or wherever a quick visual reminder might help you ask yourself, "What am I thinking right now, and are these thoughts productive?"

Moving beyond simple, personal pattern interrupt, it can be very helpful for you to define for yourself a list of "mood changers" for your classroom. It's not only the teacher's mood that effects the energy and atmosphere in the classroom. Often when kids enter a room, they bring with them the energy of playground disagreements or the energy of whatever happened in the last period. Sometimes that can be excitement and fun; sometimes it can be frustration or stress.

I have two signs on the inside of my door that are about being a champion and winning attitudes. When the students walk in the room they need to touch the signs and say out loud, "I'm a Champ!" This serves not only to ensure they have to slow down and walk through the door one at a time, but it is also a pattern interrupt for them. It may sound strange, but give it a try! If a student forgets, I simply smile and tell them, "Come back in like a champ, please!" You can download the signs from happy-classrooms.com for free if you want to try this technique. I suggest laminating the signs before putting them up. My first set got quickly stained with red/orange Cheeto stained fingerprints! I don't know who the first teacher was to use this strategy, or I would certainly give them credit. I believe it was originally used in a slightly different way by the Notre Dame football team, who touch a large "Play Like a Champion" banner before they head out to the field to play.

Strategies such as Starfish Breathing can also focus the energy of students after a short recess or lunch. But what about in the middle of a lesson when things aren't going as well as expected? Plowing through "no matter what" when it is obvious that students are not grasping concepts and are getting frustrated is never productive. Stopping, regrouping, trying something a different way is all great, but can be more easily accomplished when the air has been cleared. Scientists have determined that in as little as 17 seconds you can "change your mental channel" from being negatively focused to being positively focused. I encourage you to find some quick mood changing activities for your whole class. For me, these mood changers have changed every year depending on the personality and preferences of my class. Things they have included have been, one minute of silent ball, tossing a beach ball around the room, quick YouTube video clips ("cat fails" is always a favorite), even "academic" songs. One year I had a class whose idea of a "reward" was to sing the School House Rock learning to multiply by three song, "Three is a Magic Number!" Anything that is short, fun, positive and energizing will do. Having a repertoire of them ready and available should be an integral part of your teacher toolkit. However, it's important to balance changing the energy with learning to recognize when your class has hit the "learning wall." It took me a long time to learn that when a lesson is completely missing the mark, it will be much more productive to move on to something else entirely different and try to present the lesson again another day, in another way. The flexibility in being able to do this is one of the greatest benefits of having a self-contained classroom. I always have a chapter book that I am reading to class. Picking it up and reading a chapter is an easy way to redirect the energy.

Fake it Until You Make it

Many people underestimate the degree to which our body's physiology can affect our mood. There are three basic elements to "feeling" a certain way - our thoughts, our emotions and our physiology (what's happening physically in your body). You may notice that when people are feeling "down" their body tends to slouch, they move slower and glance downwards. Their mouth slopes down, their tone is flat and lifeless. We know how anxious people present - jerky movements, quick or shaky speech, clenched arms or nervous hands gestures or tapping feet. On the other hand, when someone is happy and relaxed their body language is generally more open, their head is raised, they smile with their mouth and their eyes.

We have known for a long time that our emotions affect our physiology. What scientists are now discovering that the inverse is also true - by changing our body's posture, we can trick our brain into changing our emotions. To avoid "cognitive dissonance" (where our brains don't match up with our behaviors) our mind can react to a physical stance and facial expression to bring our emotions in line. Basically, by changing our body language, we can also change our body chemistry.

This is good news! A powerful strategy to "change the channel" can be to simply change your body posture. If we stand up straight, relax our shoulders and smile, our emotions will more easily follow along. By making a proactive decision to act more cheerful and happy, we can release some happy hormones.

Avoid the Chronic Complainers

One essential key to staying as positively focused as possible is to limit your exposure to negative people. I have stated my case that, left to our instincts, we can all tend to veer to the negative. But I'm talking about the toxically negative people. You know who they are: the chronic complainers. People who suck the energy and joy right out of you. In recent years they have become known as "energy vampires."

Now, before I offend people, let me point out that I am not saying complaining is bad, and I'm not saying it's not valid. Goodness knows that there are plenty of problems in education right now and there is a lot of valid complaints that can be made. What I'm saying is that complaining isn't helpful. Looking for solutions is helpful, standing around "admiring the problem" isn't.

Complaining quickly takes on a momentum of its own. One person starts complaining about a student, a parent, a coworker, a new administrative policy, the next person throws in their own experiences, often with an example that is even more extreme. Suddenly the conversation is off and running, with people contributing as if it were a competition for who has it worse. It's the antithesis of focusing on what we want, and for many people, it's nothing more than a bad habit. It's a way of communicating that we've grown accustomed to and we're comfortable with. We give little thought to how it makes us feel when we're doing it. Chronic complaining not only makes us feel miserable in the moment, but it also rewires the brain to be anxious and depressed.

Complaining comes in many forms and fulfills different needs. We know that misery loves company. Some people complain to "get something off their chest." We do need to connect with people and bond over common experiences. But it's better to connect with people who are sharing the positive experiences. There are also the people who go on the search for things to complain about so that they feel justified in their dissatisfaction, unaware that they have the power to control how they react to their circumstances. Then there are those who live in "victim" mode who, no matter whatever challenges you have going on in your classroom, can one-up you and explain why they have it worse. They shoot down any solution we offer. Again, their situation is probably difficult. I'm not saying complaints aren't true or valid. I'm saying they are not helpful. It's damaging to our happiness and to the collective consciousness of the world. If we are committed to having more joy and peace in our lives, we have to make a conscious effort to limit our exposure to the complainers.

What about our conversations? Everyone should have at least one person on campus who is a "safe place" for them to share their struggles with. We need support, empathy, and suggestions. And yes, sometimes we do need to vent. It's unrealistic to think that we will never say or focus on anything that is negative. But that is different than chronic complaining.

I remember one time coming home from work and complaining nonstop all the way through dinner about a customer who had upset me. Someone in my family said, "Wow, it sounds like that person really bothers you." I answered, "He's a jerk, and he makes my life miserable!" I remember so clearly being shocked by the reality of the situation when they commented, "Then why did you invite them to dinner with us?" Think about how this applies to the staff break room at school. Who do we invite to lunch with us? We all have students that we need a precious break from, are we mentally dragging them around campus with us?

Watch Your Mental Diet Outside the Classroom

To be effective, the mindset of watching your mental diet needs to expand beyond the walls of your classroom. Again, we live in a culture that focuses on the negative. Stories of tragedy, violence, corruption, abuse, and scarcity dominate the news. I'm not saying that bad things don't happen, of course, they do. But it is hard to keep them in perspective when the media is so negatively biased. Raising my own children I reminded them many times that there is more news happening in the world than is on the television, and for the most part, the news is good. That's a basic mindset that I encouraged them to adopt.

Few people realize a belief (not a religious belief, but a belief that you have about yourself or the world) is a habit of thought. The brain seeks patterns. Once you have a belief or a repeated way of thinking, your brain will seek out evidence to support it. In psychology, this idea is called confirmation bias. You probably aren't interested in a psychology lesson, so let me approach this in the most relevant way. Either you believe the world is a good place, filled with people with good intentions: a beautiful place where bad things sometimes happen. Or you believe that the world is a hostile and dangerous place where you need to be on constant alert for bad people and bad, unfair situations. If you are feeding your mind with images of horror, negativity, and violence, it's going to be hard to maintain a positive outlook. It is the opposite of focusing on what we want.

I am not passing judgment on anyone's media consumption habits. I'm not saying watching reality TV, the evening news or following blogs aimed at sensationalizing the latest celebrity scandal is wrong in any way. I'm saying it's not a productive habit if we want a happier, less stressful life.

The world needs activists. As school teachers, most of us are answering a silent call to make the world a better place. If watching the news and seeing injustices gets you inspired to action, to work hard to make positive changes for yourself and others, then keep doing it. The world needs you. If that's the reason that you watch TV, and are constantly checking your news feed, then keep it up. But if you are participating in these activities for "fun", as a way to unwind and relax, then you need to be very picky about what you choose to passively consume. The constant barrage of commercials for beauty products, medicines and lawyers all sends us subtle messages that we are not OK the way we are and that we need to be on alert for disease and wrongdoing. The news industry is founded on the idea of journalists scouring the planet to be the first to deliver the worst things happening and then repeatedly showing them to us until another bad thing happens. Most positive or "human interest" stories are buried at the end of the newscast and only shown if there is extra time on a slow news day. I'm not saying that we don't have a responsibility to know what's going on in the world. I am just suggesting that if you want to practice being a "Joy Detective," limit your passive news and commercial consumption. As Marilyn Manson once so aptly described it,

"It's a campaign of fear and consumption."

Technology is on our side with this. With the advent of streaming services such as Netflix and many prime TV shows available "on demand," it's much easier to watch movies, documentaries and TV shows without commercials and the news. I'm certainly not above binge-watching "The Crown." I love history and science programs. But I marvel at people who can watch the 11 o'clock news as their final activity before they go to sleep. Again, I am not saying anyone's media consumption habits are wrong. I am saying they could very well be at odds with our desire for a more positive mindset. If we want to feel inner peace, watching Law & Order Special

Victims Unit is not a productive way to spend our limited "down" time.

Recap of this Happiness Mindset Habit:

Research demonstrates that approximately 70% of the thoughts we have are negatively focused. One of the keys to being happier and more relaxed is to train ourselves to focus on what we want, not on what we don't want. Avoiding negative people and conversations, and being more mindful of what we passively consume through media are practical ways to reinforce this habit. Practicing pattern interrupts and positive body posture can also be helpful tools in helping us "change the channel" of the drama playing in our brain.

Ways to Practice this Mindset Habit Starting Today:

1. Give some thought as to what your "happy place" and "happy experience" are. Complete the exercise where you describe your happy experience in as much detail as possible, using all of your senses, for at least two minutes.

2. Decide on a pattern interrupt technique to start practicing. If you decide on the "Stop, Breathe, Ask" strategy, identify your "essential question." Write the essential question or "S.B.A" on several sticky notes and post them in places that will help prompt you to use the strategy.

3. Consider downloading the "We Learn Like Champions" signs for your classroom door. You can find them at happy-classrooms.com

4. Make a list of "mood changers" for your class. If you don't know what your students love and have fun with, start experimenting with the ideas I shared in this chapter.

5. Practice your best happy/positive body posture and facial impressions in front of a mirror. It may feel uncomfortable and silly at first. I promise it won't hurt.

6. Take an inventory of the people you spend the most time with at school, and outside of school. Think about the tone and contents of your conversations with them. Do you feel optimistic and energized after spending time with them? Or do you feel that you have just participated in a pity party? If you are serious about having less stress and more joy in your life, you are going to have to take responsibility for your energy and limit your exposure to "energy vampires."

7. Remember that pattern interrupt sign on the back of your door? Every time you walk out of the door to your classroom use it as a visual clue to remember to Teach Like a Champ! What does that mean? That means making a mental note of something positive in your day so far. Maybe it's something funny a student

said, something that you are grateful for about a child or a parent or something that went well in a lesson. When you leave your room, set your intention to be a Joy Detective, and find motivating things that you like. When you run into another staff member, make sure you share the positive part of your day with them. Resolve to say only positive things about students, parents, and staff. Keep it simple. If it's not positive, don't share it.

8. Take an inventory of your media consumption. Write down all of the shows that you regularly watch, magazines and blogs that you read regularly, YouTube channels that you subscribe to. Put a "+" to media that inspires you, makes you laugh or fosters positive feelings. Put a "-" next to media that is downbeat, negative or what I would basically call "train wreck TV" (reality type TV shows that are designed to make you feel better about yourself by looking down on others - shows such as Toddlers and Tiaras, Hoarders, whatever. You know what shows I mean. You know they are going to be awful, but somehow you can't look away.) Tally the results and see if there is any room for improvement in what you are currently planting in your mind and your spirit.

"Watch your thoughts, they become your words;
Watch your words; they become your actions;
Watch your actions; they become your habits;
Watch your habits; they become your character;
Watch your character, for it becomes your destiny."

Frank Outlaw Late President of the Bi-Lo Stores (maybe)

I say "maybe," because this quote has also been attributed to Ralph Waldo Emerson, Gandhi, Lao Tzu, and Margaret Thatcher's father. If you would like to weigh in on the debate, you can find a wealth of information on this quote (and others) at quoteinvestigator.com. I know, further evidence that I am indeed a nerd. However, rest assured I make a legitimate effort to fact check quotes and research and not just grab random memes floating around social media.

Let Everyone Off the Hook

"The most important decision we make is whether we believe we live in a friendly or a hostile universe."

Albert Einstein (maybe)

I always thought this quote was from Albert Einstein. When fact-checking it appears maybe this is a misquote, taken out of context, or possibly a mistranslation. Thinking that one of the greatest genius minds of the 20th century uttered these words gives them extra validity, but no matter. I'm less concerned with who said this and more interested in its profound meaning - the world that we experience is a reflection of what we expect to find in it. Confirmation bias, again.

Dr. Wayne Dyer expressed the same idea,

> "Loving people live in a loving world. Hostile people live in a hostile world. Same world."

How does this apply to your teaching experience? Well, you can quote me on this.

> "Happy teachers have happy classrooms. Unhappy teachers have unhappy classrooms. Same kids."

You get my point. But it's not just the students. It's the same with all of our interactions. The quality of our interactions and the responses and experiences we illicit, all vary to the degree to which we are willing to let other people off the hook. What do I mean by that? Well, the degree to which we are willing to assume the best of people, assume they have the best intentions, and they are doing the best they can with the skill set that they possess.

It's a simple fact that when we hold grudges and take things that people say and do personally, we are less happy. Keeping a tally of how people have wronged us is the opposite of living a peace and joy-filled life.

As teachers, on the playground or in own class, we resolve social issues and hurt feelings for our students dozens of times a week. From simple name calling, unkind or critical comments to full-on bullying. We know the script on how to coach students. Obviously, the actual words depend on the student's age, but the script we follow more or less hits these talking points:

Young Student: "Sally said my picture is stupid."

Teacher: "Do you think your picture is stupid? It's what you think that matters. What if Sally said she hates your purple hair? Would you be upset? No. That's silly. You know you don't have purple hair, so those words don't hurt you. It's the same with your picture. You know it's not stupid, so you don't get offended."

(Note. We all have our limits. We are teachers, not superheroes after all. I understand that having repeated the same script to the same tattling student a hundred times, we're likely to resort to, "Just ignore her." There's no judgment here on that.)

Older Student: "Sally's always putting me down and saying mean things about me."

Teacher: "Sally being critical says more about her need to criticize than it does about you. That's about her, not you."

So although we are adept at coaching our students in this way, it is my observation that as teachers we often seem incapable of taking our own excellent advice. We hold on to grievances, sometimes for years. We're upset about things that another staff member has said or done to upset us. Things that a parent has said or done to offend us. In many cases, that staff member or parent did not cause offense on purpose and may even be unaware of it. In worst case scenarios, I have seen teachers in power struggles with students, being in a constant state of irritation with them, even when they are acting appropriately and performing well academically. The smallest action from the student can trigger the teacher into remembering every last annoying thing that student has ever done. There's not a lot of goodwill being thrown around; there's not too much understanding that maybe these staff members, parents, administrators, students are doing the best they can, given the skill set and the circumstances they have. Maybe, just maybe, the fact that we are constantly offended, or feel put upon says more about us than it does about them.

So this mindset is about being slower to react and take offense, and quicker about moving on when we do. Assume that others have the best intentions. Assume that no one is evil and no one got out of bed with the express intention of upsetting you. Miserable people spread misery. If someone is unkind, unhelpful, and hurtful it says nothing about us; it is merely a reflection of the dysfunction of their life. It doesn't make it right, but in many cases, it simply is what it is.

Now that's not to say that people can't genuinely hurt us knowingly and willfully. Sometimes people are plain crappy towards us. If someone has genuinely hurt you in some way, consider letting go of that grievance for the sake of your happiness. Holding onto grievances is very disempowering. Recognize that letting go of a grievance does not excuse or condone someone's behavior, it is an act of compassion towards yourself. It doesn't mean that you need to forget what a person has done, or agree with it. It doesn't mean you shouldn't take proactive action to make sure the same situation doesn't happen again in the future. Letting someone off the hook has less to do with, "Does this person deserve to be forgiven?" and more to do with, "Do I deserve to be happy?" The Buddhists have a saying,

> "Not forgiving someone is like drinking poison, and expecting the other person to die."

Holding on to a grievance hurts us, not the other person. One government study found a direct correlation between peoples' cardiovascular health and their ability to forgive. So, learning to let others off the hook is not only important to our emotional health and being happier, less stressed, and more peaceful, but also important for our physical health.

But forgiving can be hard. The deeper the hurt, the harder it is. The more time has passed, the harder it can be. What can be especially hard is when being hurt by a particular person or circumstance has become part of your "story." We live in a therapy culture. We like to identify with our pain and our sad stories. When identifying with hurt has become a habit, no matter how justified it might be, we might need to seek professional help in letting it go. Obviously, that goes beyond the scope of this book. I can't help you with that. But I do have some mindset habits to help you with that co-worker you avoid interacting with, that parent you are super critical of, and that student who bugs you. I know it's not politically correct to say that, but, again, we're human. It is entirely possible that no matter how great a teacher we are, when dealing with careers that span decades, we will all run into that one student who pushes our buttons now and again. Coincidentally, it is also the same student who is never absent. But you already knew that.

Releasing Grievances with Adults

I know of people who have held a grudge against friends, colleagues and family members for years. You probably do too. They might have held a grudge for so long that it's just become a habit. They might not even remember what the original wrong was or might be embarrassed about how trivial the original grievance was in nature. It's easy to look at others and see how destructive a habit it is. It's harder to take an honest inventory of our list of people against whom we hold grudges. I challenge you to do so now. There's a page in the workbook to help you through an exercise or grab a piece of paper. Here are some steps.

1. List the person and what specific event or comment you are holding onto that you need to release.

2. Write when it occurred. Or how often, if it's repeatedly. Try to avoid absolutes like "never" and "always." People rarely "always" do things. Be specific.

3. Weigh this incident or incidents against their positive interactions with you. List out some of the positive interactions you have had, times that you have worked well together or kindnesses you have seen them extend to other adults and children. Put it in a broader perspective of this person and their overall contribution. Do you believe that the incidents that have hurt you are representative of them as a whole? Are you focusing all of your attention on a very small fraction of their overall behavior.

4. Ask yourself honestly, "What is my responsibility in this grievance?" Is the person even aware that they have hurt you? Have you communicated to them that they hurt you in a non-confrontational way? Have you tried to resolve the issue with them in a calm and productive way? Have you taken responsibility for setting boundaries in your life so that these grievances don't happen or that people don't take advantage of you?

One of the greatest human needs is the need to be heard and understood. There is great value in "having your day in court." None of this strategy is meant to imply that you are holding on to trivial things. The grievances might be anything but trivial. The point is that holding on to them is not serving you. You have valid feelings of pain and hurt, and you want to have them acknowledged. Sometimes the simple act of letting your feelings out helps. If you don't feel you can calmly and productively confront someone who has hurt you, or if they are no longer around, write them a letter. Tell them exactly how you feel and why. You get to choose whether or not you send it. Remember, you are doing this for you, not the other person. Rip the letter up if you want, or burn it. If you find it in you to write the words, "And for all of this I forgive you" on there before you do it, you will feel better.

Releasing Resentments with Students

Let's face it; every teacher has experienced a student who bugs them. We're human after all, not saints. It's hard to "assume the best intentions" for the student who purposely goes out of their way to get attention any way they can. This can be in the form of the Class Clown, the I'll Sulk If You Don't Pick On Me Student (also known as the Professional Participant), the Constant Tattle Tale or the simply quietly (or not so quietly) defiant and oppositional student. Every classroom has a couple of these characters.

I find there are two habits here that help me out the most. Again, focus on the behavior that you want. It's not going to magically make the rest of the behavior go away, but it will help. Beyond that, it helps to have a short memory. I set a very clear intention that each block of time that I share with students they have a clean slate with me behavior-wise. I even remind them of such. I was never a teacher who had students "turn their card." If their card is turned to red by 9 AM, the rest of the day is going to follow suit. In their mind, they're already going home with a bad behavior slip, what is there to lose? I work with clips on a chart that slide up and down the behavior scale. It's fluid all day. I will tell a student, "I have a short memory. If you change your behavior after recess, I bet I'll forget all about this morning and you can slide your clip back up the scale." The point is, if a student changes their behavior, let them off the hook. Don't hold on to what they did that annoyed you earlier. Be the adult. Model the positive behavior.

Another thing that helps is to recognize that, the "worse" the behavior, the more the child is crying out for connection. There are lots of reasons that students act out that we have no control over. Some students show up to school angry or frustrated, and they have a lot in their life to be angry or frustrated about. The more troubled the student, the more they need a positive role model in their life. It doesn't always make them likable, but it makes it even more essential that we show up as our best patient and compassionate selves for them. We can be critical of their behavior, but not critical and judgmental of them. It helps to remember that we signed up for this amazing privilege and responsibility to be a teacher and to positively influence children. It often happens that the less than perfect their home life and parents are, the less than perfect their behavior is. So the irony is that the students who behave the worst, are often the ones who need us the most. Act appropriately. It helps to remember this quote by Haim G. Ginott,

"While parents possess the original key to their offspring's experience, teachers have a spare key. They, too, can open or close the minds and hearts of children."

Judge Parents Less

It's easy to be judgmental of students' parents. While many of us joke that many issues we have with "problem" students can be immediately explained once we meet the parents (as one of my colleagues very lovingly notes, "Hmm...another piece of the puzzle falls into place"), a more compassionate, less judgmental approach might serve us all better. Again, assume the best intentions. Be willing to concede that parents may very well be doing the best they can with the skills they have and the circumstances in which they find themselves.

We feel so justified in our judgment. "These parents are damaging their children!" That's our perception. But if we reverse the situation? We know how hurtful it is when the same charge is thrown in our direction, "These teachers are damaging our children!" Our defenses immediately say, "That's ridiculous, I know what's best for these kids!" Guess what? Those parents likely feel the same way. The negative energy of judgment is neither productive nor helpful.

One mindset I have found that helps put this into perspective is to remember that these parents were also once children, with hopes and dreams. Over the course of almost two decades, I have asked hundreds of children, in one form or another, what they wanted to be when they grew up. Not once did any of them ever answer, "a screw-up," "a drug addict," "a neglectful parent," "a control freak helicopter parent," or "raising kids with four baby daddies."

This point hit home for me a few years ago. Over the course of ten years, I had in my class three siblings. Well, all with the same mother but different fathers. All great kids, very different from each other, but all bringing with them the same issue - complex custody orders. The mother in this case, while always polite to me, was extremely hostile to all of her ex-partners. Very specific rules needed to be followed on what could go "home" on their "dad's night" (homework yes, backpack no). Whenever there was a meeting, a field trip, an after-school event or classrooms project that spanned any time there was a whole bunch of drama. And I mean real drama. More than once the drama culminated in threats to call the sheriff. Each time the child a helpless pawn caught in the middle.

Needless to say, I was silently judging. I wasn't judging that she had ex-partners. While having four children with four fathers is not my preference (one more sibling to look forward to!), many parents have joint custody situations and make it all work as smoothly as possible. Being one of them myself, I know it is not always easy. But I respect that the majority of parents make it as easy on their children as they can. Few classrooms these days are populated with a majority of students coming from traditional nuclear families. Joint custody arrangements are more and more the norm and in most cases sending home two copies of notes, report cards, and textbooks are all easy things that teachers are happy to do to ensure things go smoothly. So it wasn't the partners I was judging, it was the hostility shown towards them in front of her young children. I guess it doesn't matter what the situation is. You and I both have dozens of examples that we are thinking of. And what we are essentially judging people on can fall under the heading of "bad parenting."

Anyway, I was commiserating (complaining I guess) about her to a colleague who also had one of the siblings. This colleague had been at our school about ten years longer than me, and she surprised me when she said, "You know when the mother was in 4th grade she had such beautiful handwriting." It shocked me to realize that the mother had been a child too, a young student that my colleague had cared for. Probably that mother's life hadn't turned out as she had planned. When she was in 4th grade, her dream was not to be on the same campus with her young children threatening to call the sheriff.

Once I thought of her as a child, dutifully struggling to learn cursive, my judgment softened. I acknowledged that my colleague seemed to have much more love and patience in her heart for this parent and I could see that things between them generally went smoother. My judgment wasn't helping the situation. It was a powerful lesson for me.

Recap of this Happiness Mindset Habit:

To live a life with less stress and more joy, we need to be willing to assume the best of people, assume they have the best intentions, and they are doing the best they can with the skill set that they possess. Holding onto grievances and resentments is harmful to our wellbeing and our health. How people act towards us and towards others has more to do with their perceptions and state of consciousness than it does with us. Letting others "off the hook" is a positive mindset that can transform the quality of our interactions. As far as student behavior goes, often the students who behave the worst are the ones who need the most compassion and guidance from us, and it's our responsibility to rise to the occasion.

Ways to Practice this Mindset Habit Starting Today:

1. Go back and work through the steps listed above for Releasing Grievances with Adults. If you have more than a couple, chose one to tackle this week, and one next week, etc. That may not seem like a lot of

progress, but it might be more progress than you've made in a long time if these are grudges you have been carrying around for a while. You are not going to be able to forgive everyone in one day. But make a start. Additionally, commit yourself to quickly work through these steps every time a new grievance comes up, instead of letting it build up and fester.

2. If you teach elementary students, a book that is very helpful to share with class is Kevin Henkes *Lily's Purple Plastic Purse*. It's a charming story of a fidgety little mouse who causes some distractions in class with her new toys and has her precious purse taken away by the teacher. She is very upset and is as mean as a little mouse can be to her formerly favorite teacher. It's the perfect example of a teacher defusing a situation and teaching students that "Today was a hard day, tomorrow will be better." Basically, every day a new beginning. I like to share it with my students at the start of the year. And certainly there have been days I have written in my own Positive Mindset Journal, "Today was a hard day, tomorrow will be better." Don't bring today's grievances back with you to class tomorrow.

3. Remember the "day maker" calls to champion a student? Think of a parent who could do with some positive feedback and take a moment to give it to them. A quick e-mail that says, "I appreciate that Johnny always comes to school with his homework every day," or "Thanks so much for volunteering on

the field trip, I appreciated your help!" can go a long way. It doesn't need to be long, but it does need to be genuine. Think of it like writing a report card. You can always find one positive thing to say about a student, no matter what. Think about one positive thing you can say about a parent and tell them. It might be the highlight of their day. People are more self-aware than we give them credit for. Any parent who is struggling to do a good job with their child is probably aware of it. Maybe they have never received any positive feedback on their parenting. Maybe your one positive comment could be a catalyst for change for them. Maybe not. That's not for you to worry about. The point is that you extending compassion instead of criticism will be good for your well-being.

4. This strategy goes a little deeper. We're not always the teachers we want to be. You have to let that go. Again, we are human, and we have our limits. Give yourself the same leeway that you give your students. "Today was a hard day. Tomorrow will be better." Beating yourself up about it is not going to help.

5. Also, because we are often so overwhelmed and stressed, some of us engage in some pretty self-destructive behaviors. Binge watching, over eating, over drinking, overspending, zoning out on social media and internet addiction, are all ways of "going unconscious" to not deal with our unhappiness. In the next chapter, we will look at some strategies that will help you find balance in all areas of your life, and they

should help. In the meantime, I suggest you find a way to let yourself off the hook for these shortcomings, too. To gain peace and contentment with yourself, you have to be willing to forgive yourself your shortcomings. Consider writing yourself a love letter, and let yourself off the hook. It's a topic for a book all of its own, but I feel compelled to mention it here. You are going to do a poor job of loving your students unconditionally if you don't afford yourself the same grace.

Keep All the Plates Spinning

I'll get straight to it. When my life is in balance, teaching is a whole different experience. I have passion, energy, and gratitude for it. Not only do I benefit from this, so do my students. When my life is in balance, I am a better teacher, a better parent, a better partner and a better friend. When my life is not balanced, I am overwhelmed, easily irritated and drained. There is a reason that they tell you on airplanes to "Put on your own mask first, before helping others." If you don't take responsibility your well-being, you are no good to anyone else. So this mindset habit is about taking responsibility for your work/life balance, and accepting that you need to take care of yourself first.

There are times during the teaching year that your school responsibilities will be all consuming. Setting up for a new school year, parent conference week, coaching season or when you are putting on some performance or play - these are all times when you will be putting in long hours. So while there are specific times during the year that teaching will take up all of our time and energy, our job shouldn't be all-consuming all of the time. It is vitally important to take responsibility for not overcommitting and setting boundaries with our time. If we are constantly dragging around ungraded papers and teachers manuals like a pack horse and turning down social engagements on the weekend because we need to catch up on lesson planning, neglected chores or plain sleeping, it's because we have not made balance a priority. We have failed to decline and delegate appropriately. We have bought into the false idea that the needs of others are more important than our own needs. They are not. Just like our happiness, we need to take responsibility for work/life balance in our life.

I love teaching. It fulfills me on many levels, and I pride myself on being very good at it. But it's not my whole life. There are lots of things I enjoy and many other ways I feel I make contributions. And while keeping all of those in balance takes a very conscious effort on my behalf, the effort is well worth it. Keeping all the elements of my life in balance is a balancing act, much like the trick people perform of keeping numerous plates spinning in the air at the same time. While it takes discipline, it reaps huge rewards in terms of my mental and physical health, my overall life satisfaction and joy level, and the effectiveness of my results.

However, work/life balance does not happen by accident. It's not something we can buy at the store. We need to make it a priority and work diligently to ensure that all areas of our life can thrive.

One of the great benefits for most teachers is the amount of "time off" that we get throughout the year and over summer. Yes, I know summers seem to be getting shorter and shorter. But compared to most jobs where people only get two for three weeks off a year, we have a pretty sweet deal. The problem with this, of course, is that we often neglect many areas of our life during the school year, and try to play "catch up" during summer. It can often feel like once the school year gets going, we just get swept along with its frantic momentum until we arrive, exhausted, at summer break with an impossibly long list of chores and responsibilities to catch up on because we have postponed them all year. I'm sure I'm not the only person whose "summer to do list" includes personal health maintenance, car maintenance, house and yard maintenance and even a certain degree of relationship maintenance, trying to catch up with family and friends who have been neglected. That's not balance. Our life is happening now, every day, not just during summer. Delaying "balance" in our life until summer is just a different version of the unhealthy paradigm of "I'll be happy when" that I presented at the beginning of this book. And it takes a conscious effort to avoid this trap.

Here again, the first step is awareness. With awareness, comes the ability to choose differently. Many of us may be aware that we don't have balance in our lives, but find it hard to pinpoint exactly where we could make changes. I can make it easy for you. If you don't do at least one thing a day that you love doing that has nothing to do with teaching, your life is not balanced. If you don't have at least two social engagements on your calendar for the month that you are looking forward to, your life isn't balanced. If you wake up achy and feeling like you never get enough sleep, your life is not balanced.

"All work and no play" as the saying goes, "makes Jack a dull boy." I think that's an understatement. Jack isn't merely dull. He's stressed, unhealthy, irritable and not that fun to be around for his students, his colleagues, his family or his friends. Let's fix that.

Below is a quick diagnostic tool to help you get a snapshot of your current situation with regards to work/life balance

Wheel of Life Exercise

This wheel is a modification of an exercise regularly used by professional coaches. It is an effective tool to help you quickly identify areas of your life that are out of balance. It was originally developed by Paul J. Meyer, founder of Success Motivators Institute™. I have adapted it to be most relevant to your work/life balance as a teacher. This exercise only takes 10-15 minutes to complete, and it is well worth the time investment. A full sized version of the tool can be found in the Workbook.

To be of maximum benefit, this exercise should be periodically revisited, so keep a few blank copies of the wheel. It is a good practice to check in with this tool at least once a year, or after specific times when life has caused you to have to focus exclusively in one area. We all experience life challenges at certain times that will cause us to shift our priorities temporarily. There will be times when we're in transition with life situations or careers or when we are sick or injured or need to attend to sick or aging family members. At these times we can't be in perfect balance. However, having our lives be in balance most of the time will help us deal more gracefully with challenging times. Having a "road map" will also help us get back in balance sooner once the challenging time is over. So the exercise below is not designed to be done only once. It is a tool that can be completed quickly and easily any time you want to perform a work/life balance checkup.

Here are the eight areas that we will be exploring with this wheel:

- Self-Care/Physical Health
- Self-Care/Mental Health
- Fun Factor/Lifestyle
- Social Relations - Outside of School
- Social Relations - Inside School
- Purpose
- Personal Growth
- Financial Health

Here's how to complete the exercise.

1. For each question, give a score from 1-10, with 10 being the highest. Think about each question, but also go with your instinct feeling of what number comes to mind. Remember, this is not an assignment you are going to have to share or get graded on! It is a tool to help you gain an understanding of where your work/life balance currently is, and where opportunities for improvement may be. It is not a tool for you to beat yourself up with. It is a tool to help you gain clarity, and feel empowered to know where you should focus.

2. Once you have completed all 10 questions for a domain, find the average score. Round the scores up or down accordingly.

3. Place the scores on the chart with a dot.

4. Connect the dots.

5. Observe your wheel and analyze the results. How does the wheel look? Is it balanced? Are there some obvious spots where scores are low?

Here's what the blank wheel looks like. Again, it's going to be hard to write in this book, and you'll want to make a couple of copies so grab the copy from the workbook. If you are near a piece of paper now, you can jot down and figure out your numbers and complete the chart later.

School/Life Balance Wheel of Life

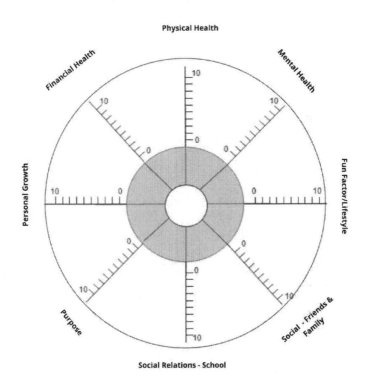

Physical Health

Financial Health

Mental Health

Personal Growth

Fun Factor/Lifestyle

Purpose

Social - Friends & Family

Social Relations - School

Self-Care/Physical Health

1. I am current with all my health check-ups, including my dentist and eye doctor.
2. I am a healthy weight.
3. I sleep without interruption 7-8 hours a night.
4. I eat 5 servings of fruits and vegetables every day.
5. I drink at least 6 glasses of water a day.
6. I get regular exercise.
7. I don't engage in excessive drinking or use of drugs (prescription or recreational).
8. I make sure I am not sitting all day.
9. I take pride in my appearance.
10. I am happy with the way my body looks and feels.

What is your total score divided by 10? Mark it on the chart.

Self-Care/Mental Health

1. I set a positive intention for my day.
2. I catch myself when I am focusing on what I don't want and choose more productive thoughts.
3. I surround myself with positive people.
4. I am present as much as I can be during the day.
5. I write down 3 things I am grateful for every day.
6. I practice Brain Breaks or meditate daily.

7. I am mindful of my mental diet and watch TV shows/read blogs/ listen to podcasts that fill me up, not deplete me.
8. I limit my exposure to TV news and social media.
9. I read something inspirational every day, even if just for a few minutes.
10. I practice positive mindsets and take responsibility for my own happiness.

What is your total score divided by 10? Mark it on the chart.

Fun Factor/Lifestyle

1. I feel I have enough free time to pursue leisure activities.
2. I have varied interests and hobbies that have nothing to do with school and students (e.g., coaching sports doesn't count).
3. I do at least one thing outside school every day that I enjoy.
4. I attend cultural events monthly.
5. I have a garden that I tend to or some other way to enjoy nature every day.
6. I take time to be playful every day with my students, my children or my pets.
7. I have dreams, and I take time to think about them.
8. I leave town on vacation at least once a year.
9. I have an outlet for my creativity.
10. I read for leisure and enjoy it.

What is your total score divided by 10? Mark it on the chart.

Social Relations (Family & Friends)

1. I engage with the family members I live with daily.
2. My family gets the best of me.
3. I talk to my family I don't live with weekly.
4. I take responsibility for my relationship with all my family members.
5. There is no-one in my family I hold a grudge against.
6. My relationships with my family and friends are rewarding and stress-free.
7. I meet/talk with my friends at least once a week.
8. My friends are a positive influence on my life.
9. My social relations leave me filled up, not depleted. (I have eliminated Energy Vampires from my social circle.)
10. I trust my family and friends.

What is your total score divided by 10? Mark it on the chart.

Work Relations (Colleagues, Students & Parents)

1. My relationships with colleagues are rewarding and stress-free.
2. I enjoy my colleagues and feel connected to them.

3. I engage in positive conversations with colleagues, not gossiping or complaining.
4. I feel I can rely on, trust and productively problem solve with my colleagues.
5. I enjoy my students and feel connected to them.
6. I feel my students respect me.
7. I feel my colleagues and administrators respect me and recognize my contributions.
8. I feel parents respect me.
9. I take responsibility for my relationships at school.
10. I respond, not react, to difficult situations adults, and children at school.

What is your total score divided by 10? Mark it on the chart.

Purpose

1. I feel my role as a teacher has purpose.
2. I feel I have a positive impact on my students and my community.
3. I believe I play an important role in making the world a better place.
4. I feel connected to something greater than myself that gives me peace.
5. I practice intentional acts of kindness.
6. I strive to positively impact every situation I encounter or interaction I engage in.
7. I view teaching more as a calling than a career.
8. I take responsibility for my job satisfaction.
9. I feel passionate about the work I do.

10. I don't need external recognition or validation to feel good about what I do.

What is your total score divided by 10? Mark it on the chart.

Personal Growth

1. I have work/life balance.
2. I have a mentor who I trust.
3. I stretch myself by mentoring someone else.
4. I continue to improve my skills so that I can be a better teacher.
5. I continue to learn skills that enrich my own life and that have nothing to do with teaching (for example, learn a new language or new hobby, learn to meditate).
6. I have goals for my life, and I am pursuing them.
7. I strive to be more present and joyful every day.
8. I am proactively learning more about myself.
9. I read and listen to podcasts/audiobooks for personal development, not just entertainment.
10. I make personal growth and increased happiness a priority.

What is your total score divided by 10? Mark it on the chart.

Financial Health

1. I have enough cash in the bank to cover 3 months worth of expenses in the event of an emergency.
2. I carry Disability Insurance and Life Insurance through my school (if offered).
3. I contribute to my retirement above what is automatically deducted for my state retirement plan.
4. I know whom to contact when the time comes to start planning my retirement (it's never too early to plan!)
5. I am educated on how years of service and supplemental educational units will affect my salary if I change school districts.
6. I regularly invest in training and additional credentials that may increase my earning potential.
7. I feel my school district pays a competitive wage and that I am fairly compensated compared to other teachers.
8. I spend less than I make.
9. I have a budget that allows for saving for things that I look forward to such as vacations and fun activities.
10. I unsubscribe from paid services I don't use.

What is your total score divided by 10? Mark it on the chart.

In the Workbook there are two samples of completed charts. Hopefully, yours looks more like the balanced one. If not, you now have some good information on where to focus your energy.

Recap of this Happiness Mindset Habit:

While teaching can be a very rewarding and fulfilling part of our life, it shouldn't be our entire life. If we focus only on our work and neglect other areas such as our mental and physical health, our social and family relations or finances, our lives get out of balance. The result is not only stress and ill health but also a lack of effectiveness. It's hard to serve others when we are "running on empty." We can use tools such as The Wheel of Life to help discover areas that have not had sufficient attention so that we can improve our work/life balance.

Ways to Practice this Mindset Habit Starting Today:

1. Complete the Wheel of Life Exercise. Remember, it's not a tool for you to beat yourself up with. It's a tool that empowers you with information so that you can make positive changes.

2. Identify areas where you can combine strategies in this book to improve your work/life balance. For example, if you have been neglecting your social relations, find ways to connect with people that also support the habit of intentional acts of kindness. Getting involved in volunteer work you enjoy will fulfill both a "social" and "purpose" need. Go online and see if you can find any local yoga, tai chi or other

mindfulness, gentle exercises classes that interest you. When you find one, see if a friend or co-worker would like to go with you. That would also support a "social" and a "mindfulness/exercise" need.

3. Set small but manageable goals that you can maintain as they become a habit. For example, if you have been neglecting your health and exercise, suddenly committing to a new diet and jogging every day may not be realistic. Set goals that are sustainable. Maybe commit to bringing your lunch from home four days a week. Commit to having one piece of fruit for recess break every day. If you wear a fitness tracker, aim to get 1,000 more steps every day. A little change, sustained, will build momentum and have more of a long-term impact than setting huge targets. It's the idea behind "habit stacking," building new, small habits that stick and together are more than the sum of their parts. It's the whole idea behind my *One New Habit* Book Series.

4. Feel some deep appreciation for your body. This ties in with mindset habit of focusing on what you want. Sure, maybe we wake up with a few aches and pains as we age, but our body is an amazing feat of nature. You don't need to be a biology teacher to be in awe of your body. Recognize that every cell in your body is both a miracle and a mystery. We have five amazing senses that help us experience the world in beautiful ways. Our 5 trillion plus cells help us breathe and

regenerate unassisted. Maybe your body has even created new life. The fact that we can move and get through most of our day pain-free is not something that we should take for granted. Once you truly appreciate your body and realize how much you enjoy feeling physically well, it's easier to make taking care of your health a priority.

5. Take an honest look at your "summer to do list" (if you are anything like me, I start compiling mine as soon as winter break is over). Is there anything on there that really shouldn't be put off until summer? I remember one year my feet started hurting in January. I relegated finding a podiatrist to the "summer list." I didn't realize how crazy that was until my son was complaining about pain in his feet. I would never have told my child I'd get to that pain in five months. Checking a few quick items off your list now will help you feel accomplished and like you are back in control of your time.

Conclusion

When talking about writing, Malcolm Gladwell, best-selling author of *Blink, The Tipping Point*, and *Outliers* points out that many people struggle with how to start their book. He suggests that if you know how you want to end your book, starting it is easy.

I always knew how I wanted to end this book. A little like *Jerry Maguire* and his famous Mission Statement, "Things We Think and Do Not Say," I want to end with a battle cry of,

"Who's coming with me?"

I believe teaching is one of the most important paths that a person can choose. I also believe it is a calling that, with the right mindset, has the potential to be deeply rewarding and full of joy. Certainly, there are challenges. But I invite us to change the narrative that we tell about teaching. Are we focused on the problems or the opportunities? Do we subscribe to the cultural stereotype of teachers being overworked, underpaid, scapegoats for a failing education system? Does the story we tell ourselves about teaching portray us as victims of a system that doesn't set us up to be successful, or as agents of change for a more positive future? The story we tell ourselves matters.

There are many aspects of education right now that are not perfect. In some ways, the world is changing faster than traditional educational establishments have been able to keep up with. We have a lot of work to do. But children are still children. What we do matters. Every interaction we have with every student matters. The more joyfully and intentionally and passionately we perform those interactions, the more likely the seeds we plant in our students will take root and play a part in them becoming healthy, productive adults. No one teaches in isolation. Whether a child is in kindergarten or in high school, each teacher relies on the teacher that precedes them and the one who will follow to provide an intertwined support system for their students. A support system that nurtures a growing child into a capable adult who has the skills and potential to impact the world in a positive and meaningful way. I thank you from the bottom of my heart for being part of that support system. Here's one final quote,

"I've come to a frightening conclusion that I am the decisive element in the classroom. It's my personal approach that creates the climate. It's my daily mood that makes the weather. As a teacher, I possess a tremendous power to make a child's life miserable or joyous."

Haim G. Ginott

Teachers make the weather. Here's to sunshine.

Additional Support

I hope you have found some strategies of value in this book. Reading about new mindset habits won't have too much of an effect on your outcomes, only trying them will. I encourage you to commit to trying the strategies that resonated with you most for six weeks. When they become a habit, incorporate a few more into your daily routines. The six weeks of journal pages should be an easy place to start.

If you enjoy the journal, there are several paperback versions available to keep you on track for an entire year. The content is the same; it boils down to a personal preference for the cover and internal graphics. You can find them on Amazon or www.happy-classrooms.com.

One Last Thing

If you enjoyed this book and found it useful, it would mean the world to me if you would leave a review on Amazon. It doesn't need to be a writing assignment, just a few sentences about what you liked about the book and who might find it helpful. Every review counts and helps this book find its way to people who may want to hear my message. Here's a direct link to the Amazon review page for digital readers. If you are reading the paperback, just find the book on Amazon and scroll down to "Leave a customer review." It could count as your intentional act of kindness for the day ☺

Reading List

Mindset: The New Psychology of Success
- Carol Dweck

Authentic Happiness: Using the New Positive Psychology to Realize Your Potential for Lasting Fulfillment - Martin Seligman

The Happiness Advantage: How a Positive Brain Fuels Success in Work and Life - Shawn Achor

The Happiness Hypothesis: Finding Modern Truth in Ancient Wisdom - Jonathan Haidt

Stumbling on Happiness - Dan Gilbert

Flow: The Psychology of Optimal Experience
- Mihaly Csikszentmihalyi

The Power of Now - Eckhart Tolle

Happy Teachers Change the World – A Guide to Mindfulness in Education
- Thich Nhat Hanh and Katherine Weare

About the Author

Grace Stevens abandoned a successful corporate VP career in 2001 to become a public school teacher, and she's never been happier. Along with two credentials to teach foreign language that she has never used, she is a Certified NLP (Neuro-Linguistic Programming) Practitioner, a closet nerd, and author of the **One New Habit** Book Series.

After living and studying in four countries, Grace settled in N. California where she currently teaches elementary school. She is mom to two amazing young adults (she may be biased) and surrogate mom to a whole bunch of eight and nine-year olds, who are also very cool. Her mission is simple - happier classrooms for teachers and students.

You can find more of her books and thoughts at:
www.happy-classrooms.com and
www.OneNewHabit.com

Made in the USA
Lexington, KY
23 June 2019